Poststructuralism: A Very Short Introduction

'Catherine Belsey guides us through the entire development
of poststructuralist ideas with brilliance, conviction, and
above all clarity.'
Alan Sinfield, University of Sussex

VERY SHORT INTRODUCTIONS are for anyone wanting a stimulating and accessible way in to a new subject. They are written by experts, and have been published in more than 25 languages worldwide.

The series began in 1995, and now represents a wide variety of topics in history, philosophy, religion, science, and the humanities. Over the next few years it will grow to a library of around 200 volumes – a Very Short Introduction to everything from ancient Egypt and Indian philosophy to conceptual art and cosmology.

Very Short Introductions available now:

Available soon:

For more information visit our web site

www.oup.co.uk/vsi

Catherine Belsey

POST-STRUCTURALISM

A Very Short Introduction

OXFORD
UNIVERSITY PRESS

OXFORD

UNIVERSITY PRESS

Great Clarendon Street, Oxford OX2 6DP

Oxford University Press is a department of the University of Oxford.
It furthers the University's objective of excellence in research, scholarship,
and education by publishing worldwide in

Oxford New York

Auckland Bangkok Buenos Aires Cape Town Chennai
Dar es Salaam Delhi Hong Kong Istanbul Karachi Kolkata
Kuala Lumpur Madrid Melbourne Mexico City Mumbai Nairobi
São Paulo Shanghai Taipei Tokyo Toronto

Oxford is a registered trade mark of Oxford University Press
in the UK and in certain other countries

Published in the United States
by Oxford University Press Inc., New York

© Catherine Belsey 2002

The moral rights of the author have been asserted
Database right Oxford University Press (maker)

First published as a Very Short Introduction 2002

British Library Cataloguing in Publication Data
Data available

Library of Congress Cataloging in Publication Data
Data available

ISBN 0-19-280180-5

5 7 9 10 8 6

Typeset by RefineCatch Ltd, Bungay, Suffolk
Printed in Great Britain by
TJ International Ltd., Padstow, Cornwall

Contents

List of illustrations

Chapter 1
Creatures of difference

A question of meaning

When Lewis Carroll's Humpty Dumpty discusses the question of meaning with Alice in *Through the Looking Glass*, which of them is right?

Humpty Dumpty engages Alice in one argument after another, just as if dialogue were a competition. Having demonstrated to his own satisfaction, if not Alice's, that unbirthday presents are to be preferred because people can have them more often, he adds triumphantly, 'There's glory for you!'

Torn between the desire to placate him and good common sense, Alice rejoins, 'I don't know what you mean by "glory".' So Humpty Dumpty explains:

'I meant "there's a nice knock-down argument for you!"'

'But "glory" doesn't mean "a nice knock-down argument",' Alice objected.

'When I use a word,' Humpty Dumpty said in a rather scornful tone, 'it means just what I choose it to mean – neither more nor less.'

1. Alice and Humpty Dumpty. Which of them is right?

'The question is,' said Alice, 'whether you can make words mean so many different things.'

'The question is,' said Humpty Dumpty, 'which is to be Master – that's all.'

Alice's scepticism is surely justified? Meaning is not at our disposal, or we could never communicate with others. We learn our native language, and in the process learn to invoke the meanings other people use. Small children find out from those who already know how to distinguish ducks from squirrels: ducks are the ones that fly. And children make mistakes: aeroplanes fly, but they are not ducks. Glory is not a nice knock-down argument.

Language makes dialogue possible, but only on condition we use it appropriately, subscribing to the meanings already given in the language that always precedes our familiarity with it. As this exchange demonstrates, there is no such thing as a private language. Humpty Dumpty has to 'translate' his before he can communicate with Alice.

Language and knowledge

Language, understood in the broad sense of the term to include all signifying systems, including images and symbols, gives us access to information. Command of a new knowledge very often amounts to learning the appropriate use of a new vocabulary and syntax. To the extent that anyone understands economics, they demonstrate the fact by using its terms and arranging them in an appropriate order. A grasp of psychoanalysis means the ability to exchange words such as 'unconscious', 'repression', or 'transference' effectively. Mathematics, science, and logic have their own symbolic systems, and qualified practitioners of these disciplines know how to inhabit them. The examination system is above all a way of policing the profession, making sure that those who qualify to join it understand how its language or symbols are conventionally employed.

Film directors and advertisers, meanwhile, know the meanings conveyed by pictures of vulnerable children or sleek sports cars. Language in this broad sense is also a source of social values. In learning to use words like 'democracy' and 'dictatorship' appropriately, for instance, Western children find out about political systems, but they also absorb as they do so the value their culture invests in these respective forms of government. For better or worse, Western children learn early on, without having to be explicitly taught, that dictatorship is oppressive and democracy so

3

precious that it is worth fighting for. In many cultures, the flag is the visual indicator of a national identity that must be defended – by force, if necessary.

Language and cultural change

If language, in other words, transmits the knowledges and values that constitute a culture, it follows that the existing meanings are not ours to command. And yet is it possible that the disdainful Humpty Dumpty has a point after all? To reproduce existing meanings exactly is also to reaffirm the knowledges our culture takes for granted, and the values that precede us – the norms, that is, of the previous generation. Examination papers in Economics, Mathematics, or Film Studies are set and marked by existing practitioners, experts in the field, whose job it is to mark down misunderstandings and misuses of the conventional vocabulary.

In this sense, meanings control us, inculcate obedience to the discipline inscribed in them. And this is by no means purely institutional or confined to the educational process. A generation ago campaigners for women's rights recognized (not for the first time) the degree to which 'woman' meant domesticity, nurturing, dependence, and the ways in which anti-feminist jokes, for instance, reproduced the stereotypes of the helpless little girl or the ageing harridan. The question feminists confronted was precisely who was to be Master, as Humpty Dumpty puts it.

In this particular case, however, his formulation was self-evidently not one we could adopt: the term 'Master' would hardly help the feminist cause, but 'Mistress' would not easily take its place, since it carried sexual connotations that detracted from the authority we were looking for. The right word in a new situation does not always readily present itself. Language sometimes seems to lead a life of its own. Words are unruly: 'They've a temper, some of them,' Humpty Dumpty goes on to observe.

In this case, the masculine and feminine values were not symmetrical – and nor, of course, was the culture. Without supposing this was the only change necessary, we none the less set out to modify the language, annoying conservatives with coinages like 'chairperson' and 's/he'. We refused to laugh at misogyny, and ignored the taunts that we had no sense of humour. For a time, dialogue did indeed become the kind of competition Humpty Dumpty's conversation exemplifies. Perhaps in a way it always is.

Language is not in any sense personal or private. But individuals can alter it, as long as others adopt their changes. What, after all, do great poets, philosophers, and scientists do, but change our vocabulary? Shakespeare invented hundreds of words. New disciplines do the same. In the course of the 20th century, science successively named 'electrons', 'protons', 'neutrons', and 'quarks'. Poststructuralism is difficult to the extent that its practitioners use old words in unfamiliar ways, or coin terms to say what cannot be said otherwise. This new vocabulary still elicits some resistance, but the issue we confront is how far we should let the existing language impose limits on what it is possible to think.

Poststructuralism and language

Poststructuralism names a theory, or a group of theories, concerning the relationship between human beings, the world, and the practice of making and reproducing meanings. On the one hand, poststructuralists affirm, consciousness is not the origin of the language we speak and the images we recognize, so much as the product of the meanings we learn and reproduce. On the other hand, communication changes all the time, with or without intervention from us, and we can choose to intervene with a view to altering the meanings – which is to say the norms and values – our culture takes for granted. The question is just the one Humpty Dumpty poses: who is to be in control?

This Very Short Introduction will trace some of the arguments that have led poststructuralists to challenge traditional theories of language and culture, and with them traditional accounts of what it is possible to know, as well as what it is to be a human being. Poststructuralism offers a controversial account of our place in the world, which competes with conventional explanations.

The importance of language

Most of the time the language we speak is barely visible to us. We are more concerned with what it can do: buy us a train ticket; persuade the neighbours to keep the noise down; get us off the hook when we've done something wrong. And yet few issues are more important in human life. After food and shelter, which are necessary for survival, language and its symbolic analogues exercise the most crucial determinations in our social relations, our thought processes, and our understanding of who and what we are.

Even food and shelter do not come into our lives undefined. Menus that offer 'succulent, corn-fed baby chicken, drizzled with a tingling lemon sauce' probably take this principle to extremes, but for me, I remember, 'scrag end stew' was a lost cause from the beginning.

Houses, too, are characterized in language, and not only by estate agents. We might want to live in one we could justifiably call old, or quaint, modern, or minimalist, but we might feel less enthusiastic once we had come to think of the same property as decrepit, poky, brash, or bleak. Paint manufacturers know that we are more likely to coat our walls in a colour marketed as 'Morning Sun' than in one called 'Custard', even when the pigmentation is exactly the same.

In this sense, language intervenes between human beings and their world. There is a party game that involves blindfolding one player as a prelude to guessing what foods are placed on his or her tongue. Whether consciously or not, guessing means classifying in accordance with the system of differences the language already provides: is it sweet or savoury? hot or cold? bland or bitter?

Poststructuralism proposes that the distinctions we make are not necessarily given by the world around us, but are instead produced by the symbolizing systems we learn. How else would we know the difference between pixies and gnomes, or March Hares and talking eggs like Humpty Dumpty, come to that? But we learn our native tongue at such an early age that it seems transparent, a window onto a world of things, even if some of those things are in practice imaginary, no more than ideas of things, derived from children's stories.

Are ideas the source of meaning, then? That was once the conventional view, but our ideas are not, poststructuralists believe, the origin of the language we speak. Indeed, the reverse is the case. Ideas are the effect of the meanings we learn and reproduce. We learned our idea of Humpty Dumpty (if we did) from nursery rhymes, Lewis Carroll, and John Tenniel, who illustrated the *Alice* books. In its account of how we become meaning animals, and the role meaning plays in our understanding of the world, poststructuralism represents a modern challenge to traditional beliefs.

Meaning

What is meaning? Where do meanings come from? Perhaps the question finds more focus in relation to a specific instance. What, then, does the word 'modern' mean in the sentence at the end of the last section? What precise timespan does 'modern' cover?

The answer seems to vary with the context. As a description of the poststructuralist challenge to inherited beliefs, it may mean nothing much more specific than 'new'. Modern history, on the other hand, generally concerns the period since the 17th century. And yet we think of modern languages as distinct from the classical languages, while modern furniture almost certainly belongs to the 20th century or later. In these instances 'modern' defines no common chronological period: modern history belongs to about the last five hundred years, modern languages to perhaps the last thousand, and modern furniture to no more than the last hundred or so. The modern challenge of poststructuralism itself is a product of the last few decades.

The term 'modern', in other words, has no positive content, but owes its meaning to difference: what is modern in these instances is respectively 'not medieval', 'not ancient', 'not antique', or simply 'not traditional'. But at least in all these cases 'modern' distinguishes a period that is more recent than another. Modern*ism*, however, denoting a style in art and literature, and associated with the first half of the 20th century, is probably no longer the latest thing, while in the compound 'postmodern', so widely used to define our own era, modernity has explicitly become, paradoxically, a thing of the past.

Nevertheless, although it seems to refer to no fixed period, we are usually able to understand and use the word 'modern' without difficulty. How? In the *Course in General Linguistics*, first published in 1916, the Swiss linguist Ferdinand de Saussure proposed that 'in language there are only differences *without positive terms*', and this observation initiated a train of thought that would be taken up by a succession of figures in a range of disciplines during the course of the following century. Poststructuralism begins with an account of how we are able to mean, and goes on to conceive of human beings as animals distinctively possessing – and formed by – this capability. We are, that is to say, creatures of difference.

Meaning, Saussure proposed, did not depend on reference to the world, or even to ideas. On the contrary. He argued that, if the things or concepts language named already existed outside

8

language, words would have exact equivalents from one language to another, and translation would therefore be easy. But as all translators know, nothing could be further from the truth. *Toto, sois sage* we dutifully intoned in my French class when I was eleven, 'Toto, be good'. But even at that early stage, we sensed that *sage* and 'good' were not always interchangeable. 'A good time' in French, we knew, would not be *sage* at all, since the term implied sense or wisdom. We were, in addition, using a mode of address that had no English translation. The second person singular that exists in so many European languages (*tu*, *Du*) can cause native speakers of English endless embarrassment when we try to communicate in other tongues, since it carries connotations of intimacy or hierarchy that can cause offence if used inappropriately.

Genders and tenses do not necessarily correspond from one language to another. 'The morning' is masculine in French (*le matin*), feminine in Italian (*la mattina*). French has the past historic, a special tense for telling stories. Some languages include more than one plural form. Differences that are given in one language have to be mastered, often with difficulty, by those whose mother tongue divides up the world in another way.

We are compelled to conclude either that some languages misrepresent the way things are, while our own describes the world accurately, or that language, which seems to name units given in nature, does not in practice depend on reference to things, or even to our ideas of things. Instead, the units that seem to exist so unproblematically may be differentiated from one another by language itself, so that we think of them as natural, just as we may perceive the continuous spectrum of the rainbow in terms of seven distinct colours.

A century ago many European nations were ready to impose their own classifications on other cultures, where imperial conquest made this possible. But the multicultural societies that have resulted from the decline of empire are willing to be more generous in their recognition of other accounts of the world, which is to say, other networks of differences.

A language represents a way of understanding the world, of differentiating between things and relating them to one another. The Kenyan writer Ngugi wa Thiong'o wrote his first works of fiction in English. Later, it came to seem to him that this practice conceded too much to the influence of the former colonial power, and the continued economic and cultural neo-colonialism of the West. However 'African' the content and themes of his early novels, the novel itself was a European genre, its structure reproducing a Western pattern of thought; moreover, the English language could not do justice to Kenyan perceptions of the world. He then began to write in Gikuyu, drawing on indigenous forms of narrative and drama.

Difference, not reference

The simple inference that meaning is differential, not referential, has profound implications for our understanding of the relations between human beings and the world, and many of them remain controversial even now. The history of poststructuralism is the story of the way Saussure's ideas were taken up by later generations, especially in France, and particularly after the Second World War, when the history of National Socialism – and of French collaboration with it – seemed to demand an explanation that existing theories of culture were unable to provide. The key term in this story is 'difference'.

Saussure and the sign

Traditionally, words had been thought of as signs. The sign seemed to represent a presence that existed elsewhere, to stand as the sign *of* something. In everyday English we still refer to the meaning 'behind' the words, as if meaning existed somewhere on the other side of speech or writing. Saussure's work changed that. For him, meaning resides in the sign and nowhere else.

In order to make the point clear, Saussure divided the sign in two: on the one hand, the signifier, the sound or the visual appearance of the word, phrase, or image in question; on the other, the signified, its meaning. In ordinary circumstances the distinction is purely methodological: we rarely see a signifier which does not signify, or mean something. But an unknown language consists entirely of signifiers in isolation. We hear sounds and assume that they signify, since we see native speakers apparently communicating, but to us they mean nothing. Or we see a page of impenetrable written characters.

If you don't happen to know Greek, this is a pure signifier:

λόγος

In its written form it makes this shape; spoken aloud, it makes a particular sound: logos. And if you do know Greek, it brings with it a signified which has no exact equivalent in English, but ranges between 'word', 'idea', 'meaning', and 'sense'. Changing the shape very slightly – and silently – by capitalizing the initial letter, we turn it into Λόγος and the signified changes to something like 'God' or 'Reason'.

Neither element of the sign determines the other: the signifier does not 'express' the meaning, nor does the signified 'resemble' the form or sound. On the contrary, the relationship between signifier and signified is arbitrary. There is nothing doggy about the word 'dog'. There can't be, since the French recognize much the same characteristics in 'un chien'. Even in languages with a shared European history, Schwein, maiale, porc, and pig have more or less the same signified. Children learn to distinguish the meaning when they learn the signifier. To use a term appropriately is to know what it means.

Grown-ups go on learning new signifiers, and the process is

> **Q. Why use the jargon term 'signifier'? Why not just say 'word'?**
>
> **A. Because words are not the only signifiers. Traffic lights, arrows, and zebra pedestrian crossings signify. So do gestures: pointing, shaking hands, punching the air. Yawns, gasps, and screams are all signifiers – in the sense that they may be interpreted by those around us, even if we didn't intend them to be. Paintings signify. Sometimes a group of words constitutes one signifier: 'How are you?' is not most usefully broken down into its component words; rather, it represents a single greeting, registers an interest – and probably *doesn't* in practice invite a list of symptoms, except in the doctor's surgery.**

nowhere clearer than in the realm of ideas. We do not have the idea of poststructuralism first, and then go on to discover the name. Instead, we learn the appropriate use of the term in the course of internalizing its meaning. 'Whether we take the signified or the signifier,' Saussure argues, 'language has neither ideas nor sounds that existed before the linguistic system, but only conceptual and phonic differences that have issued from the system.'

René Magritte's word-paintings wittily exploit the arbitrariness of the relationship between the signifier and meaning. Children used to learn to read from primers that showed pictures of things with their names underneath, to teach them what the written signifier meant. Magritte's *The Interpretation of Dreams* (1935) is composed of four such pictures, but only one of them, the valise, is appropriately labelled.

And yet, suppose 'bird' really signified 'jug'? What difference would it make?

Ferdinand de Saussure, 1857–1913

Professor of Linguistics in Paris, he moved to the University of Geneva in 1906, where he began to give the lectures that would constitute the *Course in General Linguistics* (1916). Dissatisfied with the conventional historical (diachronic) character of the discipline, Saussure chose to analyse the workings of language in its existing (synchronic) form. If objects or ideas were knowable outside the signifiers that distinguished them from each other, Saussure argued, terms would have exact equivalents from one language to another, but since translation is so often a quest for approximations, meaning must depend on difference, not on reference to things or concepts. The *Course* was put together by his students after his death. Ironically, one of the figures who exerted the most influence on what would become poststructuralism was thus not in the conventional sense the author of his own book.

Magritte places his misnamed objects against what the frame indicates are windowpanes. But these panes are painted black; the window is opaque; it does not allow us to see a world of things on the other side of it. And this is just as true in the case of the rightly named valise as it is of the other images. Both the signifier and the image are on the same side of the glass, if glass it is. Here language is not a window onto the world.

Or perhaps, instead, Magritte's window should be seen as a blackboard, traditional source of instruction about the world, where the words are chalked below the images? If so, it is surely an ironic one: the children in this class are being grossly misled.

But then again, is it ironic after all? Common sense would say so,

The door   The wind

The bird   the valise

Magritte

2. René Magritte's *The Interpretation of Dreams* parodies a reading primer. Is it also a visual-verbal 'poem'?

but common sense did not do justice to Humpty Dumpty, who turned out to have a point. Couldn't we see *The Interpretation of Dreams* as treating the words and images as two kinds of signifier: one textual, the other pictorial? Isolated visual signifiers are familiar to us, after all, in the form of road signs or brand logos. What are paintings themselves but assemblages of visual signifiers?

If we read the picture that way, we could create our own connections between the sets of signifiers in Magritte's painting. Is there, perhaps, an unforeseen parallel between time and the wind: both in flight, both imperceptible? Or could this door, half-enclosing a wistful horse, be a stable door? Is there an untold story here? The painting does not answer either question; instead, it keeps its options open or, in poststructuralist terms, preserves the secret of its final signified.

The primacy of the signifier

Poetry, too, works by proposing parallels, inviting the reader to make surprising connections between apparently distinct signifiers. Ezra Pound's delicate Imagist poem 'On a Station in the Metro' surely deserves the attention it has elicited by drawing an analogy that depends on the conjunction of unpredictability with perfect visual appropriateness:

> The apparition of these faces in the crowd;
> Petals on a wet, black bough.

And yet, you might object, these faces and petals are more than signifiers. Surely they exist, as things? We 'see' their referents in their absence, in our mind's eye, and that is the source of our pleasure in the poem?

Yes, in a way. But what the poem does is isolate these images, so similar and yet so different, from the 'noise' that would surround them in actuality. The signifier separates off the comparison it

Creatures of difference

creates from the distinct experiences as they might exist in a world of reference, and in the process produces a set of associations – the delicacy and vulnerability of faces, say – that surely relegates the reality of crowds and trees to the very edges of our interest. These associations depend (of course) on differences – between large crowds and small faces, dark boughs and pale petals, or the contrast between substantial and fragile things. Above all, there is nothing remotely referential about the strange spectrality which is the effect of the word 'apparition', before we reach the ethereal 'petals'.

That haunting quality is also an effect of the fact that we read these words as poetry: the two lines isolated on the white space of the page; the near-rhymes 'crowd' and 'bough', 'Petals' and 'wet'. Rhythm plays its part: the authority of the three last stressed syllables is contrasted with a much lighter pattern in the first line, where several short syllables are repeatedly followed by one long one.

Julia Kristeva calls this signifying capability which is not derived from the meanings of the words 'the semiotic'. It evokes, she maintains, the sound produced by the rhythmic babbling of small children who cannot yet speak. The semiotic exists prior to the acquisition of meaning, and psychoanalysis links it with the drive towards either pleasure or death. These sound effects, as they reappear in poetry, are musical, patterned; they disrupt the purely 'thetic' (thesis-making) logic of rational argument by drawing on a sense or sensation that Kristeva locates beyond surface meaning.

One more instance. William Carlos Williams's highly patterned poem 'The Red Wheelbarrow' seems to assert the materiality of the objects it names:

> a red wheel
> barrow

glazed with rain
water

beside the white
chickens

There are no comparisons this time. Instead, you might want to
insist, the poem offers the clearly defined colours and shapes of
referential things. Surely, it sets out to transmit the things
themselves to our imagination, and 'so much', it begins by
claiming, 'depends/upon' their solid existence in a substantial
world?

And yet, if we look again, there is another way to read this short,
simple text. The red and white in this poem are unqualified, and
thus bright, shiny, 'glazed'. If this is a farmyard, it is one without
shadows, or mud. Indeed, we might more readily 'see' a toy

Julia Kristeva, 1941–

Born in Bulgaria, she has spent most of her adult life in
France – as a practising psychoanalyst, as well as Professor
of Linguistics at the University of Paris VII. Kristeva estab-
lished her influence with *Revolution in Poetic Language*
(1974), which identified the radical political potential of
poetry, especially the sound patterns that disrupt linear
thought. She is a prolific writer, whose works include novels,
as well as explorations of the implications of psychoanalysis
for literature and culture. Her most influential books include
Powers of Horror: An Essay on Abjection (1980), *Tales of
Love* (1983), and *Strangers to Ourselves* (1988).

wheelbarrow, or a scene in a children's picture book. The poem seems to depict an innocence and purity not to be found on any real farm and, at least according to one possible interpretation, 'so much depends' on our ability to conceive of that lost but childlike world. Here the rhythms are simplicity itself, each short 'verse' repeating with minor variations the metrical pattern of the one before. On this reading, the red wheelbarrow of this poem issues from language, not from the world of things.

'The Death of the Author'

How can we decide which reading to settle for? Traditional criticism would say we should ask the author, and if the author is dead, as in this case, we should read biographies, diaries, or letters, until we can guess what the author might have intended. Poststructuralism, however, disagrees. If language is not ours to possess, but always pre-exists us and comes from outside, and if poems issue from language, not from the ideas which are language's effect rather than its cause, there is no final answer to the question of what any particular example of language in action ultimately means.

That does not imply, on the other hand, that it can mean whatever we like: Humpty Dumpty is wrong to think that language is entirely subject to our whim. A purely private language does not permit dialogue, and so hardly qualifies as a *language* at all. But a specific instance of signifying practice can mean whatever the shared and public possibilities of those signifiers in that order will permit.

In 1968, a year of insurrection and manifestos, when Renault workers and students took temporary control of the streets of Paris, Roland Barthes coincidentally proclaimed, in an essay which had just appeared in French for the first time, what he called 'The Death of the Author'. His argument depends on the fact that the signifier *I* is a 'shifter': it moves from speaker to speaker as each lays claim to it. In linguistic terms, the author is never more than the figure produced by the use of *I*, just as we constitute ourselves subjects of the sentences we speak by the same means. If I say 'I am hungry', I may be all sorts of other things too, but as far as the meaning of my words is concerned, I am no more at that moment than a hungry person. 'Linguistically, the author is never more than the instance writing', Barthes insists.

Roland Barthes, 1915–80

Professor of Literary Semiology (a title he chose himself) at the Collège de France. The work that made him famous was *Mythologies*, published in French in 1957 (see Chapter 2). But his most influential work of literary criticism was *S/Z* (1970), a brilliant close reading of a Balzac short story, which turns out to be much more complex – and more interesting – than we might at first have thought. His writing is always dazzling: witty, stylish, apparently mischievous and yet persuasive, serious in its implications, for all the extravagance of the manner. Among the most pleasurable of his books, *A Lover's Discourse: Fragments* (1977) offers a series of brief dramatic monologues demonstrating the tears and tantrums – and the derivativeness – of the state of being in love. Even this most individual and personal of conditions, the book indicates, is 'citational', learned from the love stories we have read or seen at the movies. 'Every other night on TV', it points out, 'someone says: *I love you*.'

Citationality

How, then, do works of art signify? By their difference, of course! It is not only at the level of the individual word, phrase, or image that meaning depends on difference. Magritte's painting alludes to old-fashioned school primers, and crucially differs from them. To see what is being 'cited' in the picture is to grasp part of what we call the 'point', which is to say, the meaning. The painting's primer does not work; its 'window' resembles and differs from the windows we know; its 'blackboard' is not an ordinary blackboard.

Moreover, *The Interpretation of Dreams* also alludes to a long tradition of Western painting, invoking the conventions of Renaissance realism in its convincing depiction of individual objects, but locating itself as modernist by putting them in unlikely places. In the same way, Imagist poems depend for their meaning not only on the combinations of individual words that compose them, but also on their intertextual allusions, resembling and yet breaking with the lyric tradition, which so often establishes a 'speaker', or at least a mood or state of mind. 'The Red Wheelbarrow' is like a fragment of a poem; on the other hand, it differs from a fragment by offering a statement that appears complete.

We should not, therefore, try to get 'behind' the work, Barthes argues. There is nothing there. Instead, 'the space of writing is to be ranged over, not pierced' (and the metaphor suggests that the quest for intention generates a kind of violence). We should look *at* the text, Barthes urges, not through it. And his manifesto concludes with a ringing declaration: 'the birth of the reader must be at the cost of the death of the Author'.

The reader

Roland Barthes wants us to read the text itself, not something else that we imagine would provide a clue to it, or a guarantee of the

> **Q. What did Barthes have against authors? Did he think books wrote themselves?**
>
> **A. He was not concerned about the author, so much as the Author. His real target was the critical institution, which maintains its control over the meaning of literary texts by making knowledge of the author's life and times the key to the only possible reading. The Author is then brought in as the explanation of the work, the final signified, closing down the possibility of new interpretations based on attention to the signifiers themselves – textual characteristics, including the story, the images, the genre, allusions to other texts, or surprising breaks with expectation.**

correctness of our interpretation. But he is not arguing for subjectivism, the view that the text's personal associations for me, as an individual reader, whatever they might happen to be, will do as an account of its meaning. Instead, his reader is not an individual, not a real person at all, but 'the space on which all the quotations that make up a writing are inscribed without any of them being lost'. Such a 'space' does not exist, except as an ideal type, a timeless, utopian, model reader. In practice, some of us will see some of the possibilities, some others, and the text itself keeps its secret about which is 'right'. Indeed, it becomes unclear just what 'right' would mean (though it's still possible, if we don't know the words, or we don't pay sufficient attention to them, or we miss a citation or mistake the genre, to be wrong).

Popular usage

Is poststructuralism just concerned with art and literature, then? A new way of approaching high culture? Not at all. Any arrangement of signifiers, it proposes, can be treated as undecidable in the same kind of way. Even the simplest instances of signification may do more work than we necessarily realize. I grew up in a world of posters which affirmed in large letters, 'Guinness is good for you!' Since I was too young to like beer in those days, I didn't give them much thought. Now, however, I wonder just what was being claimed.

It's true that stout was held to be full of nutritional value, and was often treated as a health drink, especially by middle-aged women. And Guinness was stout. But is that the whole story? The posters also showed comic cartoon animals in bright colours. Weren't these visual signifiers associating the drink with pleasure, laughter, the exchange of jokes? Weren't the adverts indicating that enjoying yourself was 'good for you', taking you out of yourself, as we might once have said? And was it the sociability of the pub, or the alcohol, that would make you see the world in the bright primary colours of the posters themselves? Either way, the claim of the images, or the words and the images taken together, was that Guinness was 'good for' your world picture, brightening the way things looked. The advertisers, I now think, were exploiting the plurality of the signifier, withholding the gratification (or do I really mean the banality?) of a final signified.

If so, the simplicity of the Guinness slogan is as deceptive as the simplicity of 'The Red Wheelbarrow'. And in both cases, the reader produces an interpretation that has no final guarantees elsewhere.

Chapter 2
Difference and culture

A world of myths

Traditional domestic cleaning products that use bleach or ammonia 'make war' on germs, or 'kill' dirt. By contrast, what was new in the imagery of household detergents, available for the first time just after the Second World War, was that they separated the dirt from the fabric decisively but without 'violence'. 'Their ideal role is to liberate the object from its circumstantial imperfection', Roland Barthes proposes, driving out alien bodies, expelling the enemy of whiteness, as it recognizes the superior virtue of washing powder. 'Their function is keeping public order not making war.' Adverts for skincare products, he argues, are 'similarly based on a kind of epic representation of the intimate', but here the moisturizers 'infiltrate' the depths and 'penetrate' the skin from outside, subverting its own propensity to wrinkle and reinstating its natural beauty.

Though Barthes does not explicitly say so, the implication is that these advertisements make their case by silently citing the imagery of the Cold War. Overt violence now gives way to a conflict based on espionage and infiltration. The political aim is to exile the left from the Free West on the one hand, and on the other to destabilize the communist states, inciting their own citizens to recognize the virtues of the free market and transform their society from within.

By drawing on the imagery of this struggle, publicity for products apparently remote from it can count on unconscious consumer recognition of the values it reaffirms.

These days, advertisers have mostly read *Mythologies*, first published in French as a book in 1957. Here, Barthes explores the implications of Saussure's account of language for our understanding of our culture. In the *Course in General Linguistics* Saussure had written:

> *A science that studies the life of signs within society is conceivable* . . .
> I shall call it *semiology* (from Greek *semeion* 'sign') . . . Linguistics is only a part of the general science of semiology . . . By studying rites, customs, etc. as signs, I believe that we shall throw new light on the facts and point up the need for including them in a science of semiology.

We probably need not take the term 'science' too literally here. In the early years of the 20th century, when Saussure was giving the lectures that would become the *Course*, science was highly valued. Any new knowledge worth its salt claimed to be a science. (At the same historical moment Freud was making identical claims for his fledgling psychoanalysis.) In any case, *science* in French is more comprehensive than in English. It tends to mean any exact or methodical knowledge, including what we think of as scientific knowledge but not confined to it.

Although *Mythologies* concludes with an essay that self-consciously sets out to develop Saussure's account of the discipline of semiology (or semiotics – the two have become virtually interchangeable), the real pleasure and interest of the book lies in its far from scientific readings of all kinds of cultural phenomena, from striptease to children's toys, from 'The Face of Garbo' to 'The Brain of Einstein'. These short pieces, originally published as journalism, set out to expose what was at stake in the representation of the everyday.

Presumably, even in 1957 most people knew that advertising was designed to sell them commodities, but what was not so immediately apparent was the citationality of this process, like the marketing of soap powders and skin creams in the vocabulary of international conflict, staged in epic terms, so that cleanliness or youthfulness also came to mean virtue. Today, when we are more alert to the way the everyday is presented to us, secondary schools teach Media Studies, which probably owes to Roland Barthes its awareness of the subtlety of the signifying practices involved in advertising, as well as its recognition that the inscription of a point of view does not have to be conscious or deliberate.

The everyday

Barthes's comments were not confined, of course, to advertisements or, indeed, to news and public events. The commonplace, Saussure's 'rites, customs, etc.', can be just as revealing. What we simply take for granted can tell us as much about our values as the opinions we deliberately arrive at after thought and discussion. Wine, steak, and *frites* all, Barthes proposes, signify Frenchness. And they bring with them, therefore, certain proprieties, a 'morality' of national identity. Knowing *how* to drink is a matter of (French) self-control; to eat steak is to assimilate (for France) a certain muscularity, blood, power.

Alternatively, why do travel guides celebrate undulating scenery as picturesque? Answer: puritanism promotes clean air and hard work. 'Only mountains, gorges, defiles and torrents can have access to the pantheon of travel, inasmuch, probably, as they seem to encourage a morality of effort and solitude.'

Sometimes, the devil is in the detail. Wolf Mankiewicz's film of *Julius Caesar* (1953) shows all the men with their hair combed forward. This lock of hair on the forehead signifies Roman-ness, and it is comic because it is so insistent, so ubiquitous. The men also sweat a good deal. This, *Mythologies* goes on to argue, signifies *thinking* (about politics). Our own values are so anti-intellectual that, by the repeated rejection of new ideas, especially new political ideas, in the name of common sense, 'laziness is promoted to the rank of rigour'. Such a world sees thought as a process unnatural enough to cause perspiration.

It's outrageous, of course. But even in translation (the selection that appeared in English in 1972 is a very *good* translation), the wit and fluency of the essays are likely to enlist a certain complicity on the part of the reader. Besides, it is always gratifying to have the sense that we see 'through' the masks and masquerades of our own culture.

On the other hand, we should perhaps beware of that 'through': there may be more meaning *in* the everyday than meets the eye but, if Saussure is right about the non-referential character of language, there are no ideas or values motivating it from outside or beyond culture itself. Culture consists of the meanings its subjects produce and reproduce. Even in the process of analysing it, we are simply taking up another position in culture, inhabiting a space culture itself provides, or can be induced to provide.

Your turn

Semiology (or semiotics) sounds easy enough, doesn't it? So do you want to try?

The passage that follows is from the first page of George Eliot's *Adam Bede*. No prior knowledge of literary criticism is required: you are a semiologist, looking for the cultural values that are affirmed or reaffirmed in the text. And remember that, to be true to Barthes, you should ignore any information you have about the author. Intention is not the issue. It might help you, though, to know that, although the story is set in 1799, the book was first published 60 years later, directly after its completion. So look out for nostalgia. And beware of the dog.

I will show you the roomy workshop of Mr Jonathan Burge, carpenter and builder in the village of Hayslope, as it appeared on the eighteenth of June, in the year of our Lord 1799.

The afternoon sun was warm on the five workmen there, busy upon doors and window-frames and wainscoting. A scent of pine-wood from a tent-like pile of planks outside the open door mingled itself with the scent of the elder-bushes which were spreading their summer snow close to the open window opposite; the slanting sunbeams shone through the transparent shavings that flew before the steady plane, and lit up the fine grain of the oak panelling which stood propped against the wall. On the heap of those soft shavings a rough grey shepherd-dog had made himself a pleasant bed, and was lying with his nose between his fore-paws, occasionally wrinkling his brows to cast a glance at the tallest of the five workmen, who was carving a shield in the centre of a wooden mantelpiece. It was to this workman that the strong baritone belonged which was heard above the sound of the plane and hammer singing –

'Awake, my soul, and with the sun
Thy daily stage of duty run;
Shake off dull sloth . . .'

As you almost certainly noticed, the passage endorses hard work. This is an idealizing picture of unalienated labour. In a village named to suggest a timeless landscape, untouched by the Industrial Revolution's dark, satanic mills, the men sing as they work, in harmony with their world. The material they shape – before the machines take over – is natural, and its scents become continuous ('mingle') with the smells of uncultivated nature in the open air. As the mantelpiece and panelling indicate, their project is the improve-ment of a home: virtuous work serves domesticity, family values.

The central figure is a skilled labourer: he is carving a coat of arms. He is also the tallest of the men. Height is a consistent signifier of authority in Western culture. And the dog that occasionally glances at him clearly recognizes its master. This is a serious, workman's dog, not the Pekinese or poodle that would denote a fop, and it is both relaxed and disciplined, which simultaneously demonstrates and justifies its confidence in the way things are.

In English fiction, dogs *know*. And this passage endorses a quintessential Englishness, evident in the name of the village (Hayslope), the materials (oak and pine), and the insistent rurality of the scene. Evidence to the contrary notwithstanding, England still *is* the countryside, and any threat to its conservation is a scandal because it threatens Englishness itself.

Nature or history?

What does this reading achieve? Does the interpretation we have produced here matter? And are the short essays that compose *Mythologies* anything more than a stylish example of Gallic wit? To explore these questions, let's look at two examples from Barthes, and some more from our own time.

First, in 'Dominici or the Triumph of Literature', *Mythologies* claims that an old French peasant was condemned to death by a form of citationality that had come to look like truth. The material evidence in the case was not clear-cut, and Dominici's trial for murder depended on psychological probability. But the psychological 'truths' that were self-evident in the courtroom were the character-types of the 19th-century novel. They were self-evident, that is, to everyone except the accused, who did not share the 'classical' literate and literary French of his accusers. In his trial, two distinct signifying practices confronted each other, each looking natural to its practitioners, but only one was supported by law and force.

28

Second, a cover of the magazine *Paris Match* showed a black soldier in French uniform saluting the flag. What did this signify? That France was a great empire, and that all her subjects, regardless of 'race', willingly acknowledged her right to co-opt their service, and indeed their lives, in her defence.

The photograph, Barthes affirms, natural-izes imperialism. Realist fiction natural-izes the belief that character is destiny, and calls this 'human nature'. *Adam Bede* shows a working man gladly and dutifully carving for someone else a family crest which denotes an entitlement to own land, and the novel thus natural-izes class difference. However sympathetic or, indeed, heroic, they may be as individuals, the deserving poor have to work for the benefit of other people – naturally.

Our own historical moment offers any number of cases where the product of history is universalized as 'the human condition'. When the Berlin Wall came down in 1989, the Free West was convinced that nature, which is to say capitalism, had reasserted itself after the unnatural imposition of communism by force, against the will of the people. Television pictures of festive crowds confirmed this view. Many in those same crowds would in due course be surprised to find that everyday life in a capitalist regime was not quite as Hollywood had portrayed it. In practice, their disillusionment with Soviet-style communism was not necessarily proof of the naturalness of the free market.

Now that the Wall had fallen, what would unite the Free West in defence of shared values? Various candidates are currently on offer. There is the threat of violence from terrorism in general and 'Islamic fundamentalism' in particular. Alternatively, for the truly credulous, there are aliens. Not unlike the old-style communist bogey, aliens tend to act by subversion and counter-espionage. They penetrate human culture and take possession of individual bodies, substituting a repulsive viscous substance for free minds, so that the possessed will involuntarily play a part in destabilizing our world.

3. Aliens. Do they unite us against a common foe? © Jacky Fleming

Or they abduct us and return us to earth transformed and incapable of defending our freedom.

Myth, Barthes explains, converts history into nature. And the task of the mythographer is to rediscover the element of history that motivates the myth, to elicit what is specific to a given time and place, asking what interests are served by the naturalization of particular convictions and values.

'Eternal Man'

In this respect, *Mythologies* indicates, our own historical moment is special. From the dirt that infiltrates our clothes to alien invasion, we have myths as never before. Why? Because the form of ownership that determines the nature of our society is bourgeois, Barthes says, and it is the particular property of bourgeois ideology to efface itself. There are no bourgeois thought-police; no one votes 'bourgeois'; the bourgeoisie simply spreads its values everywhere without naming itself as a class at all. The press, the judicial system, cookery books, weddings, and comments on the weather are all silently and anonymously informed by the representation the bourgeoisie transmits of the relations between human beings and the world. This understanding of the way things are is so pervasive that it comes to seem like a law of nature, and its hero is 'Eternal Man', a classless (and generally male) figure, who recognizes his own ideals in the norms of good sense and good taste that prevail at any given time.

Marxism and ideology

At this point in the argument, as you may have noticed, *Mythologies* has adopted a vocabulary derived from Marxism. Barthes was not himself a Marxist, but it was impossible to be an intellectual in Paris in the post-War era without taking Marxism into account. Many of the influential theorists of the time defined their own positions in

line with or against the views of the French Communist
Party.

Marxism already offered an account of culture. Karl Marx and
Friedrich Engels wrote *The German Ideology* in 1845–6, before the
revolutions that occurred all over Europe in 1848. They did not
publish this early work, which survived only in manuscript form
until the 1930s, but among all sorts of local observations, of interest
now mainly to historians of ideas, the first part in particular
includes a number of insights, not always fully worked out, but way
in advance of their time.

'Ideology', Marx and Engels proposed, consists of the forms
of social exchange that correspond to the mode of ownership
prevailing at the time. They saw history as a succession of forms
of ownership, tribal in the first instance, then 'communal' in the
city-states of Greece and Rome, next feudal, and now capitalist.
Ideology justifies the rule of each ruling class, whether as
chieftains, patricians, landowners, or those with capital, the
bourgeoisie. And in an example that perfectly anticipates
semiology, Marx and Engels point out that under feudalism we
hear a good deal about 'honour' and 'loyalty', but when capitalism
takes over, 'freedom' and 'equality' (of opportunity, presumably)
rapidly take their place.

Moreover, they argue, in order to represent its own interests as the
shared values of all members of the society in question, the ruling
class has to invest its views with the character of inevitability and
convince everyone that these ideas are the only serious option, the
one way of understanding the world that is genuinely sensible and
valid. We might now reflect on the fact that universal suffrage is the
product of the capitalist epoch. In our own period, in other words,
the mode of ownership is freely chosen, at least officially, though
always from within ideology. Capitalism becomes synonymous with
nature.

> **Q.** Isn't Marxism completely discredited now? Does anyone still take it seriously since Eastern Europe opted for capitalism?
>
> **A.** It's true that Soviet-style communism gave Marxism a bad name. But arguably those regimes owed very little to Marx's own theories, which are still unsurpassed as an analysis of the workings of capitalism. Of course, some of them need updating. But Marx has been widely read, not least by his opponents, and many of his insights have come to seem 'obvious' to us now. In my view, the Marxist theory of ideology still helps to explain why things don't seem to get better faster.

'Ideological State Apparatuses'

Under capitalism the state sets up institutions to defend property. The most obvious of these is the law, backed by the police force and the prison system. When in 1969 Louis Althusser reread (or rewrote) *The German Ideology* in the light of Saussure and semiology, as well as Marx's own later work, he began from there and went on to explain how capitalist society maintains itself. According to Althusser, the Repressive State Apparatus preserves order, the existing relations of production, in which some people have to sell their labour-power to earn a living, and some don't but live on their investments. If it is directly challenged by revolution or civil disobedience, the Repressive State Apparatus works in the last analysis by force.

But many, or perhaps most, of us barely come into contact or collision with the police and the courts. We 'work by ourselves', Althusser says, to reproduce the class relations on which capitalism depends, even if these do not serve our long-term interests. The deserving poor of the 19th century reaffirmed the values of that society, even though by doing so they mostly remained poor. Why?

Because, in Althusser's account, the Repressive State Apparatus finds a parallel in the Ideological State Apparatuses (ISAs), institutions that produce and reproduce the meanings and values which represent the relationship we imagine we have to our real conditions of existence. The ISAs tell us that work is a duty; that work well done is a pleasure; that we are free to get another job if we don't like this one; that we can move to Cuba if we don't like capitalism. (The range of places to move to is dwindling fast, of course, as McDonald's takes over the world for the free market.)

None of this is simply false: ideology is not a set of delusions foisted upon the stupid. But most of it isn't exactly the whole truth either. Being a night office cleaner, for instance, especially if you are a woman with small children, probably isn't *much* of a pleasure most of the time; what's more, without qualifications, the job you get instead might not be much better.

Althusser's list of ISAs includes religion, the family, the political system of elections and parties to choose from, the unions (in so far as they set out to improve the existing order but not to change it), the media, sport, literature and the arts, and, supremely, education. These institutions, while not homogeneous in their output, and not without internal conflict, sometimes bitter, have the effect of securing our conscious or unconscious consent to the way things are, by making them appear at best in our interests and at worst inevitable. Above all, they seem *obvious*.

In 2001 Jeremy Paxman interviewed Slavoj Žižek (of whom more in Chapter 5) on BBC radio. Žižek was calling for a radical rethink of liberal democracy. Was it, he wondered, truly 'liberal', or truly 'democratic', come to that? Could there be a better way of organizing society? Paxman could only assume that Žižek must want to go back to East European communism. What else could

Louis Althusser, 1918–90

Professor of Philosophy at the École Normale Supérieure in Paris. Althusser reread the works of Marx in the light of 20th-century theoretical developments, including linguistics and psychoanalysis.

In *For Marx* (1965) he put forward the theory that society could best be understood as working on three levels: economic, political, and ideological. Each of these levels had a degree of independence, or 'relative autonomy', but each was also the condition of existence of the others, though they would not all necessarily move at the same rate. The motor of change was contradiction in or between the three levels. In line with Marx's own view that the form of ownership defined social relations, Althusser maintained that the economy was determining 'in the last instance'. But conversely, the economy could never be finally isolated from the other two levels, so 'the lonely hour of the "last instance" never comes'. The ideology that did most to sustain capitalism was humanism, the belief in 'man' as the free, autonomous origin of history.

His essay 'Ideology and Ideological State Apparatuses' was published in 1969. This developed the attention given to ideology in *For Marx*, seeing it as the means of reproducing the relations of production (class struggle).

In 1980 Althusser murdered his wife and was subsequently confined to a psychiatric institution. His autobiography, *The Future Lasts a Long Time* (1992), tells his version of the story.

there be? This was an instance of ideology at work: capitalism is better than communism, obviously, *and the idea that there might be an alternative to both is apparently unthinkable.*

Those of us who were involved in teaching in the 1970s, when Althusser's essay on the ISAs first appeared in translation, were thrilled to learn that the education system was the main ideological apparatus. This meant that, as radicals, we had work to do on our own doorstep, instead of looking slightly out of place on other people's picket lines. The argument was that schools and universities not only eject a proportion of the young prepared to take up occupations at every level of the economic structure, but in the process of teaching reading, writing, and arithmetic they also provide instruction in obedience, deference, elementary psychology (the character-types of the 19th-century novel, for instance), the virtues of liberal democracy, how to give orders, and how to serve the community. In short, educational institutions inculcate discipline, and the self-discipline that encourages their pupils to go out into society and 'work by themselves' to maintain the status quo.

A more recent example would be the demand (with the best intentions, of course) that sex education should always be given in the context of family values. The family, we know, is yet another place where children are supposed to learn obedience, deference, and the values (especially the heterosexist and gender values) of their community. (The reality, we are beginning to recognize, may be rather different. Besides love, the family can also shelter domestic violence, sexual abuse, and untold psychological torment.)

Ideology secures the system by consent. It is not a conspiracy. Its reaffirmation is not deliberate. Adam Bede doesn't set out to reproduce the existing class relations. On the contrary, he simply does his duty and takes pleasure in his work. But it is exactly the sense of duty and pleasure that mask the element of exploitation involved in the fact that he has to sell his labour-power (he can't

36

afford not to) for a wage that is less than his employer will get for the coat of arms he is carving, and much less than its purchasers probably earn from the rents they impose.

Adam Bede doesn't set out to mask exploitation either. But by showing the scene in its ideal form, and presenting class difference as inevitable, obvious, this 'realist' novel does in practice reproduce the imaginary relations of individuals to their real conditions of existence.

The subject

Does this mean that George Eliot should be roundly condemned for colluding with exploitation? Of course not. The moral praise-and-blame school of literary criticism (just *how* anti-feminist was D. H. Lawrence? how anti-Semitic was Shakespeare?) has not taken account of the Death of the Author. George Eliot is not the origin or the explanation of the cultural convictions her novel reproduces. Besides, the novel is remarkably sympathetic towards its working-class hero. The text is an effect of the meanings and values in circulation at its own historical moment.

Adam Bede (who does not exist), George Eliot (who is not Adam Bede's origin), and the unsuspecting reader (the one who has not carried out a semiological analysis) participate in a shared practice which reproduces the ruling ideology. These three figures are all, Althusser would say, subjects.

The subject is in the first place the subject of a sentence, the agent of a verb, and the figure that says 'I'. I reproduce (or challenge) the ruling ideology when I speak or write, and I am in that sense a source of initiatives, actions, decisions, choices. But at the same time the subject is *subjected* to the meanings and sentence structures that language permits. I communicate *subject to* my reproduction of the accepted signifiers. We might want to argue (though Althusser doesn't explicitly) that the subject is condemned

Q. Isn't this a bit depressing? It makes us all out to be no better than conditioned robots. We might just as well be possessed by aliens after all.

A. It does imply that we're not necessarily the sole origin of our deepest convictions. But we can make choices and our views can change. How? It's the *ruling* ideology that confirms the way things are. Althusser's essay is mainly about the workings of ideology in general, but specific ideologies can challenge the ruling values (Marxism for one, poststructuralism for another). We don't have to insist on what's obvious. Indeed, the obvious is often incoherent when you try to think it through. Contradictions in the ruling ideology produce new beliefs, alternative subject-positions. (There will be more to say about dissent in Chapter 5.)

Running through the ISAs essay is a series of references to class struggle. As a Marxist, Althusser took for granted that all societies divided by class (which is to say, all societies hitherto) are propelled forwards by conflict, including theoretical disagreement. He wanted to privilege Marxism itself as a source of truth, so he called it 'science'. But a certain anxiety about this term pervades his work in its entirety. He was too good a philosopher to suppose that you could combine certainty with Saussure. Ideology itself is always a site of struggle.

So, incidentally, is the subject. How coherent are your beliefs and values? Have you never found you subscribed to two beliefs which can't both be true?

to citationality. The ambiguity of the subject's status, as agent and as subjected being, defines the use of the term.

The subject, Althusser maintains, is the destination of all ideology, and the place where it is reproduced. This is the source of its power: ideology is internal; we are its effects; we cite it unwittingly every time we reaffirm the 'obvious'.

Ideology or myth?

Clearly, there is considerable overlap between what Barthes calls 'myth' and what Althusser means by 'ideology'. Which term should we adopt?

'Ideology' indicates a Marxist allegiance. But because the same signifier is in common use to define a consciously held doctrine ('conservative ideology'), rather than what is, on the one hand, so obvious that it goes without saying and, on the other, the location of incoherences, contradictions, and political struggle, it is often necessary to explain how you are using the word before getting on with the argument.

Moreover, not all Marxists agree about its definition. Before Althusser published his essay, 'ideology' was commonly equated with 'false consciousness'. In Althusser's writings, the boundary between true and false is not so clearly marked. Ideology may present an 'imaginary' picture of the relations of production, but because it is lived in our everyday experience, it is not simply a delusion which can be shaken off once we recognize the truth. And how, in the light of Saussure's account of language, could we be sure it *was* the truth, anyway?

'Myth', too, is equivocal. Greek myths are fictions, we would now say. But we might also recognize that they were attempts to make sense of the world. Myths are not just for entertainment, but stories of the origins of things. For the culture that subscribes to them, they have explanatory power.

Roland Barthes's use of the term was a tribute to one of the major intellectual figures of the time, certainly the greatest mythographer of his generation, the anthropologist Claude Lévi-Strauss. Rejecting the ethnocentrism characteristic of an earlier generation of anthropologists, Lévi-Strauss refused to think of tribal cultures as 'primitive'. On the contrary, what interested him was the meaning of their customs, and the common ground between their everyday practices and ours.

Take the widespread tribal custom of *potlatch*, for example, where gifts are exchanged between families or communities. Each gift is expected to be more lavish than the previous one, until finally one side in the exchange gives away everything, leaving the other in sole possession of the field. This, Lévi-Strauss suggests, has parallels in the modern Western Christmas, where the quantity and the value of the cards received, and ritually exhibited on the mantelpiece during the festival, testify to the recipient's worth. Presents are expected to reach a certain standard (children become adept at exploiting the competitive element here), and at the end of the holiday many family budgets are in a state of 'disequilibrium'.

This example comes from Lévi-Strauss's first book, *The Elementary Structures of Kinship*, published in French in 1949. Here, he argues that all societies have rules about who can marry whom, so that their members are divided into two categories: prohibited partners and possible partners. Marriage within these rules constitutes a fundamental form of exchange, and the project of exchange itself is 'reciprocity' as a way of overcoming hostility. Reciprocity means communication, alliance, integration, society itself. *Tristes Tropiques* (1955) includes analyses of aspects of Amazonian art and ritual to show how they are intelligible to the ethnographer in terms of the local marriage rules.

To the ethnographer, but not to the practitioners themselves. Like Barthes's *Mythologies*, which appeared in 1957, Lévi-Strauss's structural anthropology focuses on motivations that escape the gaze of the individuals concerned. It is not, he affirms, impossible for practitioners to become aware of the implications of their own practices, the rituals and myths that cultures re-enact and reproduce, but such awareness represents the exception rather than the rule. Similarly, we may assume that the French do not necessarily choose steak to affirm their national identity: probably, they just like the taste. But the taste, as Roland Barthes would say, is not the whole story.

Anthropology offers a solution to the problem of terminology. In the end, its topic is neither mythology nor ideology, but culture. That signifier is not without its problems too, of course, but it has the effect of implicating us all in the common practices of our society,

Claude Lévi-Strauss, 1908–

Professor of Social Anthopology at the Collège de France 1959–82. Lévi-Strauss, who claims to have chosen ethnography in order to avoid philosophy, became a professor at the University of Sao Paulo in Brazil in 1935. From there he did the fieldwork among the native peoples of South America that provided the material for his books. The most influential of these include *The Elementary Structures of Kinship* (1949, second edition 1967), *The Savage Mind* (1962), and *The Raw and the Cooked* (1964). *Tristes Tropiques* (1955) is a unique work, part autobiography, part travel writing, and part non-technical anthropology, by turns witty and haunting, always eloquent and thoroughly readable.

His efforts to evade philosophy were not entirely successful. Treating institutional and cultural differences as reducible to binary oppositions inscribed in the mind, his writing ultimately proposed an account of human nature itself.

which are neither true nor false but carry meanings and values we may not have chosen consciously.

Structuralism or poststructuralism?

Were Barthes and Althusser simply applying the findings of structural anthropology to their own culture, then?

They certainly borrowed its account of determinations that escape our conscious awareness, but there is at least one crucial difference. In looking below the surface appearance of things, Lévi-Strauss wanted to find the common element of all cultures, traceable ultimately to universal structures embedded deep in the human mind. Thus, all myths are in the end transformations of each other, and all marriage customs reducible to the great duality of the incest taboo, where 'incest' is marriage with a forbidden spouse, and everyone is either a potential partner or a prohibited one. The founding principle of human culture in general is exchange, transforming hostility into reciprocity.

His quest, in other words, was for Eternal Man, that fantasy figure of bourgeois ideology, the single, continuous hero of history masquerading as nature. Structuralism was extremely seductive: it was speculative and far-reaching; it promised a key to all human practices; it offered mastery of the single principle that would hold together the apparently disparate features of all cultures. But it treated difference as no more than superficial, and difference was the key term in Saussure's revolutionary theory of language.

During the heady days of the 1960s, structuralism was everywhere. It moved easily from myth to stories. Barthes himself produced an essay on 'The Structural Analysis of Narratives'. In 1928 the Russian Formalist Vladimir Propp had analysed the fairy tales of his own culture, ignoring the variables to find a single structure of 7 possible characters and 31 possible actions. *The Morphology of the Folktale* first appeared in English in 1958, eliciting an essay from

Lévi-Strauss in 1960. This essay praised Propp's work, but pointed out that the problem with formalism was its policy of ignoring thematic content. When in 1966 A.-J. Greimas published the ambitious *Structural Semantics*, he brought together Saussure and Lévi-Strauss to rewrite Propp for structuralism. What he found was a pattern for all stories, centring on the conflict between the hero's quest for individual freedom and the constraints of the existing order.

At just that time, Jacques Derrida wrote critically about the nostalgia Lévi-Strauss displays for a lost human wholeness, as well as the binary oppositions his case both depends on and fails to sustain. But perhaps the most explicit textual moment of poststructuralism came in 1970 at the beginning of *S/Z*, Roland Barthes's anarchic, infinitely suggestive, and still unsurpassed close reading of Balzac's short story, 'Sarrasine'. Apropos, apparently, of nothing in particular, *S/Z* begins, 'There are said to be certain Buddhists whose ascetic practices enable them to see a whole landscape in a bean.' This rumination then continues:

> Precisely what the first analysts of narrative were attempting: to see all the world's stories (and there have been ever so many) within a single structure: we shall, they thought, extract from each tale its model, then out of these models we shall make a great narrative structure, which we shall reapply (for verification) to any one narrative: a task as exhausting (ninety-nine percent perspiration, as the saying goes) as it is ultimately undesirable, for the text thereby loses its difference.

Suddenly, the grand claims of structuralism appear absurd. Once you have found the single determining structure, there is nothing to choose between the universe and a bean. The microcosm simply becomes an illustration of the general pattern, another instance of the same – thrilling for the system-builders, but then what? What can further investigation discover? Only endless repetition. The big questions have been answered in advance.

How ironic, then, Barthes goes on, that Saussure's attribution of meaning to difference should lead in the end to the equalization of all texts 'under the scrutiny of an in-different science' (in-different because undifferentiating, but also indifferent because in the end apathetic, bored).

When *S/Z* itself sets up five 'codes' as the universal framework of its textual analysis, the process suggests a parody of structuralism, not least because the brilliant 'divagations' (wanderings) of *S/Z*'s own analysis keep on leaving them behind. At the same time, these purely formal codes set out to specify a set of relationships between the text and the reader, and within them Balzac's story is shown to have some quite remarkable themes, which are certainly neither universal nor eternal.

Is *Mythologies* poststructuralist?

If Barthes's *Mythologies* belongs in a line of descent from structural anthropology, is it right to class it as poststructuralist? In so far as the question matters at all (and perhaps in the end it doesn't, much), my answer would be yes and no.

Lévi-Strauss looked, he said, for the invariant element among superficial differences. To a degree, Barthes does that too: the confusion of nature with history is a recurring theme. But this theme is not itself universal or invariant. On the contrary, it belongs specifically to our own bourgeois moment, and has nothing whatever to do with structures deep in the human mind.

Besides, *Mythologies* frequently seems to forget that this is its topic. Though the essays are all to varying degrees sceptical about the myths they analyse, and interested in drawing surprising parallels, they are not concerned to reduce them to a single theme. In one case in point, Barthes contrasts Audrey Hepburn with Greta Garbo. Garbo's face, still, white, perfect, like a mask, resembles the timeless Platonic ideal of beauty as it exists in the mind of God. Hepburn's

4. The sculpted face of Garbo.

charm, by contrast, is individual, expressive, characteristic of its time in the 1950s.

And so, the essay concludes, 'The face of Garbo is an Idea, that of Hepburn an Event.'

5. Audrey Hepburn. An Event . . . ?

Lévi-Strauss based his analysis on binary oppositions: the raw and
the cooked, the legitimate and the forbidden, nature and culture,
hostility and reciprocity. 'The Face of Garbo' replicates these
dualities by contrasting the two stars. And if it cheekily links this
antithesis to a distinction, common in Western culture and derived
from Plato, between the timeless and the transitory, the essay makes
this binary opposition as an ironic comment on the way we reduce

diversity to order, rather than the declaration of a universal truth which the instances exemplify.

What is more, the contrast marks a transition in the history of cinema, and perhaps in our ideals of beauty. Garbo's face, Barthes claims, begins to approach the moment when awe gives way to charm, a change that is completed by Hepburn. In other words, if the 'universal' is ironically invoked, this is in order to make a point that is local and historical, not the other way round. The contrast is also sharply observed in its particularity. Lévi-Strauss's method, then, is used, but in order to draw attention to historical and individual differences.

The influence of Saussure is perceptible in Lévi-Strauss, but it is by no means pervasive. Conversely, Saussure seems to propel Barthes away from depth and universality towards the contingency of history and the specificity of the signifier. Towards, that is to say, difference.

And Althusser?

What about the ISAs essay? Is that structuralist, or poststructuralist? This much more abstract thesis concerns ideology in general, with examples drawn from bourgeois ideology. Here again a case could be made either way. But what points forward in Althusser's work is the element of struggle involved in constantly renewing (reproducing) the obviousnesses that sustain the existing relations of production. Education may be the most powerful of the ISAs, but even here there are teachers who (heroically) resist promoting what is reactionary in the curriculum.

It is implicit in Althusser's analysis that ideology is divided against itself. And if ideology is in this sense *other than it is*, so is the subject which is its effect and support. The subject, then, is our next concern.

Chapter 3
Difference and desire

Death in Paris

In a miserable lodging house in February 1868 Abel Barbin died of carbon dioxide asphyxiation by means of a charcoal stove. Abel, who was 29 years old and worked in a railway office in Paris, left a memoir which testifies both to his high intelligence and to the desolation that led to his suicide. It appears that he was caught between two jobs, neither of which matched his abilities or took account of his experience. Friendless in the capital and frequently unemployed, convinced that he had no chance of the companionship and sexual satisfaction marriage would offer, he saw his existence as useless to others and crushing to himself.

Abel, who was baptized Adelaide Herculine Barbin, had grown up as a girl. She had spent most of her life in all-female institutions and, after coming top in the examinations, had gone on to teach in a girls' boarding school. There she fell in love with a woman teacher, gradually recognizing, to her own surprise, the nature of this passion, which was consummated in due course. The two shared a bed for many months, until the suspicions of those around them, and the falseness of their position, prompted Adelaide Herculine to consult a priest, who passed her on to the medical authorities. The doctor found a person of slight but broadly masculine appearance, with rudimentary versions of the genital organs of both sexes. There was no womb.

In 1860, at the age of 21, Adelaide Herculine was re-registered officially as Abel, and lived from then on as a man. The early parts of the memoir, somewhat literary and sentimental, nevertheless clearly depict a girlhood of relative social integration and considerable academic success. In telling Abel's story, however, the text becomes rambling, repetitive, and sometimes incoherent. Even so, it is clear that Abel feels alone and disgraced, unable to return to those who have known him as a woman. More aware, now, of what is expected sexually, he sees no hope of a future relationship to match the first. Meanwhile, the jobs he applies for all demand experience. Abel's experience has been as a schoolmistress, but at this time a career as a teacher in a girls' school was not an option for a man. Hungry, he is reduced to asking his poverty-stricken mother for money. This, we may construe, is still more humiliating for a son than it would be for a daughter.

Socialized, culturally constructed in a world where sexual roles were dramatically polarized, Herculine/Abel cannot survive as either a woman or a man. Having been recruited as a woman by the meanings of femininity she has done her best to inhabit, she cannot simply become a different, masculine subject, sharing and reproducing the meanings that make possible male bonding and conventional male behaviour.

The polarity between the forms of subjectivity appropriate to men and women could hardly have been more extreme than in mid-19th-century bourgeois and provincial France. It is easy to see, though the author of the memoir cannot theorize it, how difficult it would be, both socially and psychologically, to become a member of the opposite sex in such circumstances.

Virginia Woolf made high comedy out of the reverse transformation in her novel *Orlando* in 1928. Waking up to find herself suddenly, as if by magic, a woman, after growing up as a man, Orlando has to learn to cope with the difficulty of getting around in skirts, retreating where she has been accustomed to pursue, choosing whether to yield or refuse when she has previously learned to insist. Now she finds that women are not 'obedient, chaste, scented and exquisitely apparelled by nature'. Instead, they can only acquire these virtues 'by the most tedious discipline', and Orlando reluctantly sets about the task.

Herculine Barbin's predicament was no joke, however. It was not eased by the insistence of her priest and the medical profession that she must be reassigned to her 'true' sex. Sexually relaxed though we seem to ourselves to have become, our own society still does not feel comfortable with intersex babies, and the doctors generally take it upon themselves to determine the 'true' sex of such children, often, if the 'adjustment' is minor, without consulting their parents. Western culture decrees that there are two sexes; the English language, as the inscription of a culture, offers two pronouns, one masculine and one feminine, and subjects are expected to identify with one or the other. The most scrupulously non-sexist parents have no choice but to speak of their children as 'he' or 'she', and children generally do their best to become what language tells them they are.

Brought into line

We are now more open to the possibility of same-sex relationships or, indeed, bisexuality. But the idea that an act is *either* homosexual *or* heterosexual, that a person is gay, straight, or *bi*sexual, only confirms that we think in terms of two sexes and two subject-positions, one of which must be appropriate in every case. 'I' is often ungendered, but in most European languages, when people speak about themselves, they match the pronoun with either masculine or feminine adjectives.

These days we are less inclined to dress our babies in *either* pink or blue. Plenty of yellows and greens are available to sidestep the issue (though department stores still stock pretty pink dresses and jaunty blue romper suits). But if women wear unisex trousers without comment, men in skirts can still raise eyebrows. Though things are changing fast, certain behaviours, attitudes, and values continue to be thought of as predominantly masculine or feminine.

Free subjects?

Gender-identification is one instance among many of the fact that people in liberal societies are free subjects, entitled to speak and write, to proclaim their views, however eccentric, and to challenge the existing order if they wish, but only on condition that they also subject themselves to certain culturally defined norms. Of course, anyone can always refuse to conform. But outright refusal often gets people labelled as freaks or loonies, and correspondingly discredits the challenges they deliver in the eyes of those they address them to. The man in a suit commands assent more readily than the homeless bag-lady shouting at the traffic.

In the memoir, though it was literally Abel who did the writing, the narrative voice that recounts the convent girlhood is not characteristic of a man. Lives are narratable as coherent in terms of the categories language makes available. The story of Herculine, as told by Herculine herself, makes sense. But at the point in the story when she ceases to be the subject language and culture have made of her, the writing collapses into incoherence. Neither a woman nor a man, in the sense that Abel has no male experience, habits, bonds, ways of thinking of himself, or in short, no *history*, this newly created subject can say 'I', but without being able to attach to it an intelligible sentence beyond something like ' . . . am poor, lonely, and very unhappy'.

Identity can be conceived of as a set of psychological characteristics, or as a social role, as recognition of the appropriateness to oneself of a classification, or as membership of a group. In all these senses, Abel has lost one identity without managing to find another. Giving priority to language in the construction process, poststructuralism thinks in terms of grammatical categories and talks about subject-positions. The subject of a sentence is the person (or thing) who enacts the verb: 'Abel looked for work'. A subject takes a position by uttering, even if silently, a sentence using 'I': 'I want a job'.

As a free subject, I plan my life (within certain obvious constraints), affirm my values, choose my friends (if they'll have me), and give an account of myself: 'I am . . . this or that'. But I do so on condition that I invoke (*subject* myself to) the terms, meanings, categories that I and others recognize, the signifiers we have learned in the process of learning our native language.

Q. Isn't the term 'subject' redundant, when we already have 'identity'?

A. 'Subject' can be more precise than 'identity' as a way of thinking about the issues. First, as a grammatical term, it places the emphasis squarely on the language we learn from birth, and from which we internalize the meanings, including the meanings of 'man' and 'woman' our culture expects us to live by. Second, it builds in the ambiguity of the grammatical term itself: I am free to say and do what I like to the degree that I accept a certain subjection to those cultural norms. And third, it allows for discontinuities and contradictions. I can adopt a range of subject-positions, and not all of them will necessarily be consistent with each other. 'Identity' implies sameness: that's what the word means. Subjects can differ – even from themselves.

Foucault

Michel Foucault, who collected the documents concerning Herculine Barbin, devoted most of his work as a historian of ideas to analysing the effects of culture in permitting us to give an account of ourselves. The categories we all recognize not only make this account possible, but also *call us* to account, and by doing so bring us into line with the norms and proprieties that culture itself constructs. Societies recruit us as subjects, subject us to their values, and incite us to be accountable, responsible citizens, eager, indeed, to give an account of ourselves in terms we have learned from the signifying practices of those societies themselves.

Foucault's *Discipline and Punish*, first published in French in 1975, considers the ways in which societies have penalized those who rejected their norms. In absolutist France, for instance, criminals were publicly tortured and executed, and the book begins with a detailed and thoroughly gruesome account of the punishment of a regicide in 1757. Foucault immediately juxtaposes this with a list of regulations of an institution for young offenders in the mid-19th century. The rules prescribe the exact distribution of their time: up at six; five minutes to dress in silence; another five to make their beds; work until ten and then a meal, after washing their hands; school at twenty to eleven for two hours; and so on, until bed-time at half-past eight. If the public execution was a spectacle in which the state demonstrated its cruel power to punish those who challenged the sovereign, the institution looks more humane, more lenient, and more constructive. And so, of course, in an obvious sense, it is. But its agenda is a discipline that subjects the inmates, body and soul, to a regime designed precisely to construct them as conforming citizens, which is to say *subjects*, in both senses of that term, who learn to work by themselves in submission to the values of their society.

Resistance

Which of these two regimes allows more scope for resistance?
Ironically, the first, Foucault argues. Punished in public, criminals
who behaved courageously sometimes became popular heroes.
Ballads were circulated giving their side of the story. Crowds
occasionally turned on the executioner. But hidden away and
trained to internalize new disciplines, prisoners were more
effectively brought into line, to emerge as docile subjects, the fight
drilled out of them.

All relations, Foucault argued, are in this sense relations of power.
Parents and teachers subject children when they socialize them.
Professions set exams and in the process define the knowledges
required to join them. Anyone who tells or shows anyone else how
to do something is exerting power over them. This is not a matter of
intention or wish. The transmission of knowledge involves
instruction; learning entails submission.

Norms, then, are culturally produced and, to the degree that they
exert a discipline, represent a form of oppression. In Foucault's
account, power is creative: it produces ways of being and ideals to
aspire to. His last two books, contributions to the massive history of
sexuality he planned but never completed, analysed the classical
'arts of love' that provided codes for the intensification of pleasure
by the construction of an 'ethics' of conduct. The 'good' life recruited
subjects as if for their own benefit, inciting them to internalize a
discipline that invisibly subjected them to its account of what
constitutes the good. Every morality, regardless of its content,
Foucault argues there, consists of two elements that belong
together, 'codes of behavior and forms of subjectivation'.

But does this mean we cannot resist our own subjection? No, of
course not, though there might be a price to pay. There is by
definition no power without the possibility of resistance, Foucault
insists, and the word carries heroic overtones for a generation that

remembered with admiration the dangers incurred by the refusal of the French underground to submit to the German occupation. Resistance is power's defining difference. Crime itself is a refusal of the law; eccentricity is a repudiation of norms; 'vice' is a rejection of conventional ethics. Power is not a thing or a quantity we possess or lose, but a relation of struggle. Foucault's own work is full of doomed heroes: murderers, madmen, and suicides who struggled against their own subjection. His life, especially latterly, was lived beyond the limit of respectability. He died of AIDS.

Sexual 'norms'

Among Foucault's most influential propositions was the argument put forward in the first volume of *The History of Sexuality* that homosexuality did not exist until the 19th century.

But surely the Greeks practised homosexuality? Not exactly, Foucault would reply. Certainly, men had sexual relations with boys or men, just as they have done in many other cultures. But they were not in consequence classified as homosexuals, invested with a subjectivity that was seen as the origin of their sexual practices, and regarded as deviant or perverse. The Greeks did not consider themselves in any way defined by their sexual habits.

The effect of the relatively recent process of classifying sexual subjects, Foucault indicates, was twofold. On the one hand, it tended to limit the range of available forms of pleasure. Once you feel an obligation to come out, if only to yourself, to *decide* whether you are gay or straight, you declare a preference that constrains your choices, however unconsciously. On the other hand, as soon as the category exists, you can identify with it, and then defend it, insist on your rights, and join forces with others who feel oppressed by the norm, invoking what Foucault calls a 'reverse discourse' as the basis of resistance to the norm itself.

Michel Foucault, 1926–84

From 1970 Professor of History of Systems of Thought at the Collège de France. His studies of madness, medicine, punishment, and sexuality had in common a preoccupation with the power relations involved in the control of what constitutes reason, knowledge, and truth.

In Foucault's account, things generally start badly and get worse. Our own more humane forms of discipline recruit subjects more effectively than overt displays of power. Graeco-Roman civilization recommended the care of the self as a way of enlisting subjects, but since the Enlightenment a bleaker 'self-knowledge' has taken the place of this ideal.

Resistance, however, is the inevitable corollary of power, he affirms, the difference without which it has no meaning.

Psychoanalysis

Poststructuralism is not a system, nor even, when you look at the details, a unified body of theory. How could it be? Its key term is difference.

Louis Althusser, who urged that, as the destination of ideology, subjects 'work by themselves' to reproduce it, unless they deliberately resist, was a Marxist. Michel Foucault, who broadly agreed with Althusser's account of the subject, rejected Marxism as another kind of 'discipline', a self-proclaimed 'truth' that recruited subjects to its own norms. Foucault was deeply suspicious of all such truths. On similar grounds, he also deplored psychoanalysis, because it co-opts us in the name of the truth of our innermost being, understood to be sexual. It was, after all, the reassignment of Herculine Barbin to her 'true' sex that destroyed her.

Foucault's is a familiar way of reading Freud, but not the only possible one. Post-War Paris was a place of many rereadings. If Roland Barthes reread Lévi-Strauss in the light of Saussure, Althusser even more explicitly reread Marx in the light of psychoanalysis to produce his account of ideology. But his version of psychoanalysis was already itself a Lacanian rereading of Freud. No wonder no one agreed with the exact details of anyone else's view!

Jacques Lacan did not promise the truth, nor did he see sex as the origin of identity, but he did reinterpret Freud in the light of Saussure (and Lévi-Strauss) to delineate a subject which was itself the location of a difference. Lacan's subject is divided against itself; 'other', he says, 'than it is'; dissatisfied – and desiring.

The subject of desire

Why is it that the big love stories, those that become legendary when so many are forgotten, tend to be the ones with unhappy endings? Most people in Western culture probably know the stories of more than one of the following: Dido and Aeneas, Antony and Cleopatra, Tristan and Isolde, Lancelot and Guinevere, Romeo and Juliet, Anna Karenina, *Gone With the Wind*, *Brief Encounter*, *Casablanca*. (Do you? How did you score? Two is promising; five is good; all nine and you could write a book.)

Why do we remember them? Why have some of the oldest ones been recycled so many times in opera, novels, and films? Is it that unfulfilled desire for some reason strikes a particular chord? Lacan would say so.

For Lacan, the human being is an organism-in-culture, and the disjunction that implies is the source of all our troubles. We are born organisms (of course), and we become subjects. How? By internalizing our culture, which is inscribed in the signifying practices that surround us from the moment we come into the world. We turn into subjects in the process of learning language, which means that we become capable of signifying. This is an advantage: we can ask for what we want instead of crying helplessly, and go on to catch the right bus, write emails to our friends, make political speeches – or read Lacan, of course, according to taste.

But the language that permits all this is irretrievably Other. Lacan uses a capital O to distinguish the Otherness of language and culture from the otherness of other people, though of course it is from other people that we learn and internalize the Otherness of the signifier. They, too, however, are its products.

The big Other is there before we are, exists outside us, and does not belong to us. In the course of asking for what we want, for instance, we necessarily borrow our terms from the Other, since we have no alternative if we want to communicate. In this way, the little human organism, which begins with no sense of a distinction between itself and the world, gets separated off from its surroundings and is obliged to formulate its demands in terms of the differences already available in language, however alienating these might be.

Something is lost here – experienced, perhaps, as a residue of the continuity with our organic existence, or as wishes that don't quite fit the signifiers that are supposed to define them. Lacan calls what is lost the real. The real is not reality, which is what culture tells us about. On the contrary, the real is that organic being outside signification, which we can't know, because it has no signifiers in the world of names the subject inhabits. The real, repressed because it has no way of making itself recognized in our consciousness, returns to disturb and disrupt our engagement with a reality that we imagine we know. Unable to use the existing language, the lost real makes its effects felt in dreams, slips of the tongue, puns, jokes, or symptoms marked on the body, illnesses or disabilities that seem to have no physiological cause.

The general effect of the lost but inescapable real of our organic being is a dissatisfaction we cannot specify. A gap now exists between the organism and the signifying subject, and in that gap desire is born. Desire, Lacan says, is for nothing nameable, since it is unconscious, not part of the consciousness language gives us. But it is structural, the consequence of the gap that marks the loss of the real, and thus a perpetual condition. Although desire is unconscious, most of us find a succession of love-objects, and fasten our desire onto them, as if they could make us whole again, heal the rift between the subject and the lost real. In the end, they can't – though, of course, it's possible to have a good time in the process of finding that out.

Prohibitions

Lacanian psychoanalysis takes from Freud the idea of the forbidding Father (with a capital F, because this figure is a structural position rather than the actual person who romps with the kids or helps them do their homework). Lacan is enough of a Freudian to retain the idea that children want *everything* (including their mothers). The lynchpin of the culture they must learn to obey is the Father, who says 'no' to most of what they want (especially their mothers). Lacan inscribes this point in a pun that works only in French. When we learn language, we submit to the *Non/Nom* that the Father bequeaths us, his 'no', as well as his name.

In a sense, 'good' subjects take on both, inheriting the Father's values along with his name, which is to say, we take up a place in society on condition that we reproduce its signifying practices, derived from the big Other. Lacan calls this the symbolic order: 'symbolic' because signifiers are symbols; 'order' because language is a discipline that recruits and forbids in one breath.

Venus

Lacan would have approved of Titian's Venuses. I once went to an exhibition of Titian's paintings, with no particular expectations,

6. The goddess of love is subject to desire.

except that it would be pleasurable. In the event, I walked slowly round the gallery in a daze, came out at the end of the exhibition, and immediately joined the queue to go round again. I had never seen so much desire in a single space. Even the portraits seemed to stare wistfully out of the canvases, at an angle to the spectator, as if they could see something in the distance that they couldn't have and we couldn't name.

Venus Blindfolding Cupid shows the goddess of love punishing her son for shooting his arrows apparently at random. Ironically, her action is only likely to make things worse: a blind Cupid will surely act even more anarchically. But Venus does not appear to be concentrating on her task. She looks off to the left, apparently at nothing in particular, her expression suggesting that her daydream does not give her much satisfaction. Meanwhile, the other winged putto looks sadly over her shoulder, perhaps pitying Cupid, or possibly foreseeing his own fate.

Maybe Venus herself is the victim of Cupid's arrow here. It wouldn't be the first time. In Shakespeare's narrative poem *Venus and Adonis*, she falls in love with the beautiful but indifferent Adonis, who prefers hunting. The poem draws attention to the paradox of her role: 'She's love, she loves, and yet she is not loved'. As the goddess of love, Venus is not only the supreme object of desire, but its subject too, capable of more than mortal longings. The poem ends by making the story into a fable of the origin of desire's pain. Disappointed, Venus curses love, and as the personification of the condition, she has the power to make her curse come true. From now on, she announces, passion will always be full of anguish.

Lacan thought so too. There is, he insisted, no such thing as perfect sexual rapport. But the desire he saw as an inevitable component of the human condition was not necessarily erotic. In Lacanian theory it is not some fundamental sexual imperative that motivates desire, but the loss of the real, which leaves an incompleteness, a lack. We can see, Lacan argues, how sexual relationships come to 'occupy' the field of desire, since they involve the signifier at its most lyrical, as well as the organism at its most sensitive, but they are not its source. Indeed, they are not its

Jacques Lacan, 1901–81

Psychoanalyst who radically reinterpreted Freud in the light of linguistics and anthropology. His *Écrits* (1966) are extraordinarily elusive, cryptic, and dense at first reading. Lacan's annual Seminars, conducted in Paris from 1953–4 onwards, have been gradually appearing in print, first in French and then in translation. These are less obscure, but only marginally so.

The writings and these oral deliveries were addressed to psychoanalysts, whose job it was, Lacan believed, to listen extremely attentively to what their patients said. The role of the analyst is to hear the voice of the unconscious, which makes itself audible through the censorship of consciousness in riddles, allusions, elisions, and omissions. Lacan's own riddling manner mimics the utterances of the unconscious.

For his admirers, the style makes his texts themselves into objects of desire. 'This time,' I always think, 'I'm going to get it straight.' If only.

But it becomes easier. And it is worth it. Lacan was enormously well read and highly intelligent. His incidental comments on painting, architecture, tragedy, for instance, are often worth whole volumes of more ponderous scholarship.

solution either, since the signifier and the organism often pull in different directions.

Perhaps in the end the most compelling passion, the one that is never satisfied, is the desire for knowledge, the longing to push back the limits imposed by the symbolic order.

Strangers to ourselves?

Facing exile, Thomas Mowbray in Shakespeare's *Richard II* complains that in a foreign country his tongue will become like a musical instrument that has lost its strings.

Julia Kristeva's book *Strangers to Ourselves* is about foreignness. It begins with a moving, poetic account of what it's like to be an immigrant, cherishing 'that language of the past that withers without ever leaving you'. You improve your skills in the new language, but it's never quite *yours*, and you lack the authority that goes with unthinking fluency. You are easy to ignore, and thus easily humiliated. Increasingly foreign to those you have left behind as well, you become a kind of cultural orphan, never *at one* with anyone anywhere.

At the same time, immigrants may suddenly find the prohibitions they have grown up with suspended as the power of the symbolic order is lifted. They become 'liberated', other than they are. But are they freer? Or just more solitary?

Why do we fear foreigners, people from other cultures, asylum seekers? Well, for one thing, they demonstrate that there are alternative ways to be, that our own ways are not inevitable, and therefore not necessarily 'natural'. Disparaging the others seems to make some people feel better. Besides, the encounter with foreigners calls into question the 'we' that is so easily taken for granted.

This badly needs to be called into question, Kristeva concludes. Psychoanalysis indicates that we are all foreign to ourselves. In the first place, there is something everyone has left behind:

> A child confides in his analyst that the finest day in his life is that of his birth: 'Because that day it was me – I like being me, I don't like being an other.' Now he feels other when he has poor grades – when

he is bad, alien to the parents' and teachers' desire. Likewise, the unnatural, 'foreign' languages, such as writing or mathematics, arouse an uncanny feeling in the child.

And in the second place, we are all inhabited by a stranger, whose ways are unknown to us, and contest the values we (think we) take for granted:

> The foreigner is within us. And when we flee from or struggle against the foreigner, we are fighting our unconscious – that 'improper' facet of our impossible 'own and proper'.

In these circumstances, one object of desire, especially familiar in a colonial and postcolonial world, is identity itself. Many people, especially those subject to a history of imperial oppression, experience a longing to belong. And who, in a globalized world, is not at the mercy of institutions, corporations, a language defined or controlled elsewhere? Since the 19th century, nationalism has offered to restore a true identity that has been all but erased.

Jacques Derrida considers this issue in *Monolingualism of the Other*, first published in French in 1996. His own special case is French Algeria, where he grew up as a Jewish child in the 1930s. Ironically, Arabic was taught in the schools there as if it were a foreign language. Hebrew, meanwhile, was not taught at all. French was the young Derrida's first language, although this too was the property of others: it belonged in the faraway country of France.

And yet, in a sense, Derrida argues, his own case was exemplary for all of us. Culture is always 'colonial', in that it imposes itself by its power to name the world and to instil rules of conduct. No one inhabits a culture *by nature*. As a matter of definition, no culture comes naturally. We are all exiles. Moreover, the culture we belong to is never beyond improvement, never quite what it *should* be.

Don't nationalists identify with the nation as it once was, or as it one day might be? Isn't perfect identity always the property of others?

At the same time, in the current world order we do well to remember that not all exiles are politically equivalent. Some people are more exiled than others . . .

Scandal

With Kristeva's proposition that we none of us know quite who we are, with Derrida's affirmation of our inevitable exile, Lacan's view that our dissatisfaction is structural, and Foucault's emphasis on resistance, poststructuralism has tended to have a certain radical edge. But no aspect of it has been more scandalous than its account of the subject. Constructed to a high degree by the big Other, subjected by meanings outside its control and even its consciousness, divided against itself as the effect of a loss, the subject of poststructuralism is neither unified nor an origin, and is thus a far cry from the unique individual who has traditionally represented humanity in the Free West. Western institutions, electoral systems, and the economy all assume that human beings are the independent source of meanings and choices. The freedom prized so highly is freedom to be whatever consciousness makes of us. In other words, Western 'common sense', itself a cultural construct, conspires to convince us that we are what we think.

The belief goes back nearly four centuries to René Descartes, the philosopher who affirmed, 'I think, therefore I am'. In a quest for the ultimate truth, Descartes set out to strip away any beliefs he could not be certain of. He was left with one conviction which, he claimed, could not be doubted: that, as the person doing the doubting, he at least must exist. On that basis, he was able to rebuild a philosophical system which, he insisted, owed nothing to outside authorities.

The Cartesian *cogito* played a major part in promoting the scientific and rational development of the Enlightenment in the 18th century. These days, most philosophers would have some reservations about Descartes, but his famous phrase has become part of current Western common sense. Its effect is to conflate the self with what thinks. 'I' become primarily a consciousness, and that consciousness, in turn, is seen as the origin of 'my' ideas and values.

Poststructuralism, I have already suggested, questions the view that consciousness is an origin, treating it rather as an effect of signification: I owe to the big Other the meanings and differences that permit me to think at all. Psychoanalysis deepens the scandal by redoubling consciousness with unconscious processes that exercise other determinations, according to an agenda we don't even recognize. The free individual is no longer either individual or free.

Mind and body

Descartes believed that, whereas he *was* a mind, he *had* a body. The two were radically distinct from one another. The organism had its own mechanical processes and reflexes, but reason was wholly independent of physiology. If we now take for granted that psychological tension causes headaches, or stress affects our immune system, we owe that recognition in part to psychoanalysis, which as early as the 1890s began attributing physical symptoms to unconscious desires.

But psychoanalysis does not on that account settle for the idea that a human being is best understood as an undifferentiated 'whole'. On the contrary: the relation between the organism and the subject is an uneasy one, to the degree that we become subjects at the price of an organic loss. This loss is not simply a single event in the past, but repeats itself throughout human life, and we subsist as an uneasy conjunction of organic impulses and cultural values, each at the expense of the other.

The term 'subject', then, is not just a jargon word for 'self'. While what we mean by 'the self' (or 'person' or 'individual') is generally the whole package, the subject is divided both within itself and from the organism. As what speaks or writes, the subject is, on the one hand, conscious (rational, deliberate), and on the other hand, unconscious (motivated by desires that make themselves known only indirectly in dreams, slips, jokes, or symptoms). What is more, unconscious desires frequently conflict directly with conscious wishes: that is why they are not admitted to consciousness. Meanwhile, this composite subject is inseparable from the body – when the organism dies the subject ceases to exist – but at the same time, it is distinguishable from the body, if only to the extent that each is conceivable only at the price of the loss of the other. As pure organism, I would not be a subject. At the same time, I cannot ever be pure subject, because I remain an organism.

We are born human beings, in that we are the offspring of two human parents; we become subjects as a result of cultural construction *and* what culture represses, namely, the lost but inextricable real.

It's a hard life

With all these divisions in place, it's not much fun being a subject, at least some of the time, for any of us. No wonder, then, that Abel Barbin decided he had had enough.

Herculine's body was more masculine than feminine; but as a subject, her cultural construction was more feminine than masculine. Falling in love, bringing the subject and the organism into joint action, created a crisis. Assigned to what the doctor called his true sex on the basis of his body, Abel was required to create a new subjectivity overnight. It couldn't be done, and he became confused, incoherent, depressed. If psychoanalysis is right about the unconscious, we none of us know quite what we mean when we say 'I'. Abel had this problem to the power of ten. Life in such circumstances seemed unliveable, and he put an end to it.

Oppositions

As the last paragraph makes particularly clear, using the oppositions the symbolic order provides makes some things impossible to say with any accuracy. We cannot do justice to Herculine/Abel's story in terms of the names or pronouns on offer. How should we name this figure who, to compound the confusion, calls herself Alexina in her memoir? And should we say 'he' or 'she'? 'his' or 'her'? I have uncomfortably used the feminine forms for the early life and the masculine forms for the period after the reassignment. But the two stages were not in practice as clearly distinct as that.

The hermaphrodite, Jacques Derrida might say, deconstructs the opposition between masculine and feminine, just as psychoanalysis, I would want to add, deconstructs the opposition between mind and body.

But deconstruction is another story, and deserves a new chapter, beginning with the relationship between difference and truth.

Chapter 4
Difference or truth?

Objective knowledge?

Jeanette Winterson's novel *Written on the Body* has an unnamed narrator whose gender is never revealed. Since this is a love story, the question is, you might think, material. The other central figure is a woman. Is this relationship heterosexual or lesbian? The novel doesn't say, though it drops hints that point sometimes this way, sometimes that.

Some readers, resisting the Death of the Author, argue that since the book is written by a woman, the narrator must be a woman. They presumably ignore the fact that 300 years ago Daniel Defoe impersonated a woman in *Moll Flanders*, or that substantial parts of Dickens's *Bleak House* are recounted by Esther Summerson. Emily Brontë, meanwhile, included narrators of both sexes in *Wuthering Heights*, beginning by impersonating Mr Lockwood. The difference is that in the modern (or postmodern?) novel, we can't be sure.

Sometimes it's genre that's in question. Toni Morrison's *Beloved* centres on a woman whose dead baby returns to disrupt her world. Are we to take this child's existence literally, or is she a psychological projection, a way of acknowledging the implications for the African-American present of the unresolved past of slavery? Is the novel psychological realism, in other words, or a ghost story? Or is it, conversely, a more thought-provoking work if we don't decide?

At the end of the 20th century, a whole succession of Hollywood films took as their theme the question of the difference between fiction and reality. Was there one? Could we be certain where the boundary lay? In particular, Peter Weir's *The Truman Show* (1998), *Pleasantville* (directed by Gary Ross, 1998), and David Cronenberg's *ExistenZ* (1999) focused on that issue, without necessarily resolving it. Might we interpret such a concentration on this question as a cultural symptom? In *Last Action Hero* (directed by John McTiernan) Arnold Schwarzenegger plays the fictional hero, Jack Slater, who returns to 'our' world to rescue Arnold Schwarzenegger from death at the première of his own Jack Slater movie. But this was 1993, and Arnie's fans were not yet ready for a postmodern plot that queried what was real, not to mention a film that depended on allusions to Shakespeare's *Hamlet* and Ingmar Bergman's *The Seventh Seal. Last Action Hero* has since become a cult classic.

In posing the question of the difference between fact and fiction, without resolving it in order to deliver the 'truth', popular culture came into line with the implications of Saussure's insights into language as I outlined them in Chapter 1. If language is differential rather than referential, if we owe our ideas of things to differences which are the effect of language in the first instance, then we can never be certain that what we say about the world in language or, indeed, in any other signifying system, is true.

In other words, if the source of our perception of differences is signifying practice, not things in the world, there are no guarantees that our account of it arranges the world of things accurately. The most familiar notion of truth is the idea that what we say corresponds to the actual state of affairs. But how, independent of the signifier, can we ascertain the state of affairs itself? If different languages divide the world up differently, and if different cultures lay claim to distinct beliefs, what, apart from habit, makes 'ours' more true than 'theirs'? Moreover, an increasingly multicultural West has come to acknowledge, however grudgingly, that other cultures do arrange things differently. Racism feeds on the widespread anxiety that, if other cultures manage with other world pictures, our own may not be as authoritative as we like to think.

This is not to say, of course, that Jeanette Winterson, Toni Morrison, and a succession of Hollywood directors had all diligently read Saussure or the poststructuralists, though it's possible. A more likely explanation is that, as so commonly occurs in the history of culture, a number of causes converged to 'overdetermine' (the word comes from psychoanalysis, but was given new currency by Althusser) this uncertainty about what we (think we) know. Throughout the 20th century new theoretical developments, including sociology, ethnology, and psychoanalysis itself, combined to indicate that beliefs might be the effect of motivations we do not necessarily recognize.

The issue here is not what exists, but what we can accurately *say* exists. Faithful to Saussure, poststructuralism is concerned with what goes on in language. Truths (or otherwise) are told in language. Poststructuralists don't (normally) doubt that there is a world: their anxiety concerns what we can claim to know about it with any certainty.

Many people today are willing to surrender the idea that there is in all instances a single, authoritative truth to be discovered and defended. Indeed, a century of political groups not only defending the truth as they perceived it, but initiating devastating violence against people who didn't share their convictions, has left many of us ready to have serious doubts about the assertion of truth claims. Besides, travelling the global village, even if only on television or the Internet, we encounter a wide range of world pictures. The young, in particular, are often willing to give up on truth.

The subject to the rescue?

But a common alternative is to hold that 'it's all subjective', or that truth exists as the property of the individual. 'It's what I believe', people say; 'it's true for *me*'. By this means they lay claim to a proper tolerance of other opinions, but at the same time they manage to hold on to the view that the individual consciousness is the place where ambiguities are resolved. If unmediated and unmotivated access to objective facts is not an option, truth, they assume, must be a purely personal matter.

The poststructuralist alternative

Poststructuralism looks at the question differently. In the first place, if the subject is an effect of culture, a result of the circulation of meanings in the symbolic order, rather than their origin, subjectivity is more likely to reproduce the uncertainties and the range of beliefs we encounter than to resolve them. How many people do you know whose opinions are all entirely clear-cut and, at the same time, compatible with each other? Are your own views wholly consistent? My friend Susan's aren't, despite her best efforts. She has no religious convictions, because she doesn't see any reason to believe in the supernatural. At the same time, she's very reluctant to walk under ladders and always reads her horoscope.

And in the second place, the distinction between the subject in here and the object out there is itself the consequence of the old view of the relationship between human beings and language. If, in the Cartesian tradition of the Enlightenment, my consciousness is what exists unconditionally, and language is no more than the instrument it makes use of to communicate about the world with other consciousnesses, we can conceive of knowledge in terms of a subject contemplating the objects it knows about. On the other hand, if our consciousness is itself brought into being by borrowing meanings from the big Other, and if the world itself is differentiated by language, we cannot any longer think in terms of a binary opposition between a knowing subject in here and the objects of its knowledge out there.

Truth and knowledge exist at the level of the signifier. In other words, truth is a matter of what we can say (or write, or indicate in diagrams or chemical symbols). If we lay claim to the truth, whether we conceive of this as objective or subjective, we are drawing on the big Other to do so. We are defining what we believe, that is to say, in terms drawn from out there, however much we seem to feel it in here.

To that extent, what we believe is no longer purely personal, but a conviction that culture permits (even if that same culture also deplores it). How many of the beliefs we experience as 'subjective' are in practice culturally inculcated?

Deconstruction

Poststructuralism claims that the conventional antithesis between subjective and objective doesn't hold, because the subject is produced outside itself. It does not make sense to isolate the subjective, since the subject originates nothing, and we cannot, therefore, appeal to the subject as the absolute origin of its own views. Views are learned from somewhere, even if we cannot remember where or when, and even if we are the very first person to bring together separate views to make a new one. At the same time, there is no purely objective knowledge, because knowledge is necessarily the property of a subject. A fact may exist for ever, even if the human race dies out, but knowledge of it doesn't go on without a subject there to do the knowing. What is outside the subject constitutes subjectivity; the subject invades the objectivity of what it knows.

If you've followed that argument this far, you have just carried out the process that Jacques Derrida identifies as deconstruction, analysis of the inevitable invasion of the other into the selfsame.

Jacques Derrida, 1930–

Born and brought up in Algeria, Derrida moved to Paris at the age of 19 to complete his education. There he has taught successively at the Sorbonne, the École Normale Supérieure, and the École des Hautes Études. He is also Professor of Philosophy and Comparative Literature at the University of California, Irvine.

His first book was on Husserl's geometry (1962), but *Of Grammatology* (tr. 1976), *Speech and Phenomena* (tr. 1973), and *Writing and Difference* (tr. 1978) were all published in Paris in 1967. Since then he has written extensively on language, art, ethics, and politics, experimenting with typography and finding inventive ways to break with linear prose.

Of his many books, my personal favourite is probably *The Post Card: From Socrates to Freud and Beyond* (1980). The first half of *The Post Card* is a love story, told in letters (or on very large postcards!), in which the object of a forbidden, impossible desire, it finally turns out, is (probably) metaphysics.

The work that first made Derrida's international reputation was *Of Grammatology*, which appeared in French in 1967. The topic – writing – appeared uncontroversial, and the title scarcely seemed to herald a blockbuster. And yet *Of Grammatology* delivered a resounding challenge to the entire tradition of Western philosophy, and although the book has been endlessly misread, misquoted, and denounced, its arguments have not so far been effectively refuted.

what, after all, of the remain(s), today, for us, here, now, of a Hegel?

For us, here, now: from now on that is what one will not have been able to think without him.

For us, here, now: these words are citations, already, always, we will have learned that from him.

Who, him?

His name is so strange. From the eagle it draws imperial or historic power. Those who still pronounce his name like the French (there are some) are ludicrous only up to a certain point: the restitution (semantically infallible for those who have read him a little—but only a little) of magisterial coldness and imperturbable seriousness, the eagle caught in ice and frost, glass and gel.

Let the emblanched [*emblémi*] philosopher be so congealed.

Who, him? The lead or gold, white or black eagle has not signed the text of *savoir absolu*, absolute knowledge. Even less has the red eagle. Besides, whether *Sa* is a text, has given rise to a text, whether it has been written or has written, caused writing, let writing come about is not yet known.

Sa from now on will be the siglum of savoir absolu. And IC, let's note this already since the two staffs represent each other, the Immaculate Conception. A properly singular tachygraphy: it is not first going to dislocate, as could be thought, a code, i.e., what we depend [table] on too much. But perhaps, much later and more slowly this time, to exhibit its borders

ensigned is not yet known. Perhaps there is an incompatibility (rather than a dialectical contradiction) between the teaching and the signature, a schoolmaster and a signer. Perhaps, in any case, even when they let themselves be thought and signed, these two operations cannot overlap each other [*se recouper*].

Whether it lets itself be assigned [*enseigner*], signed,

Its/His [*Sa*] signature, as thought of the remain(s), will envelop this corpus, but no doubt will not be contained therein.

remain(s) to be thought: it (ça) does not accentuate itself here now but will already have been put to the test on the other side. Sense must conform, more or less, to the calculus of what the engraver terms a counterproof

themselves: two passages.

This is—a legend.

Not a fable: a legend. Not a novel, not a family romance since that concerns Hegel's family, but a legend.

The legend does not pretend to afford a reading of Hegel's whole corpus, texts, and plans [*desseins*], just of two figures. More precisely, of two figures in the act of effacing

"what remained of a Rembrandt torn into small, very regular squares and rammed down the shithole" is divided in two.

As the remain(s) [*reste*].

Two unequal columns, they say distyle [*disent-ils*], each of which — envelop(e)(s) or sheath(es), incalculably reverses, turns inside out, replaces, remarks, overlaps [*recoupe*] the other.

The incalculable of *what remained* calculates itself, elaborates all the *coups* [strokes, blows, etc.], twists or scaffolds them in silence, you would wear yourself out even faster by counting them. Each little square is delimited, each column rises with an impassive self-sufficiency, and yet the element of contagion, the infinite circulation of general equivalence relates each sentence, each stump of writing (for example, "*je m'éc . . .*") to each other, within each column and from one column to the other of *what remained* infinitely calculable.

Almost.

Of the remain(s), after all, there are, always, overlapping each other, two functions.

The first assures, guards, assimilates, interiorizes, idealizes, relieves the fall (*chute*] into the monument. There the fall maintains, embalms, and mummifies itself, monumemorizes and names itself—falls (to the tomb(stone)) [*tombe*]. Therefore, but as a fall, it erects itself there.

1

Difference or truth?

7. **Derrida breaks with linear prose in *Glas*.**

Binary oppositions

Western culture, Derrida argues, depends on binary oppositions. In this respect the structuralists were heirs to 25 centuries of thought. Moreover, these oppositions are always hierarchic. One term is highly valued, the other found wanting. Nature is privileged over culture, just as speech is privileged at the expense of writing. But these terms can never sustain the antithesis on which they depend. The meaning of each depends on the trace of the other that inhabits its definition.

Deconstructing Lévi-Strauss

Of Grammatology included a close reading of Lévi-Strauss. In *Tristes Tropiques* Lévi-Strauss recounted what he called 'A Writing Lesson'. The Nambikwara tribe watched the anthropologist making notes and attributed power to the process of writing. When Lévi-Strauss gave them paper and pencils, the Nambikwara soon learned to make wavy lines on the page, presumably in imitation of the practice they had witnessed. But their Chief saw an additional possibility here. With a view to impressing upon his own people his participation in the secrets of the white man, he pretended to read out his own scribbles. The episode prompts Lévi-Strauss to reflect on the implications of literacy. In accordance with the Western tradition of treating writing as secondary, the transcription of speech, and thus 'fallen' from the grace of a purely oral culture seen as closer to nature itself, Lévi-Strauss aligns writing with exploitation and violence. The ethnologist blames himself for destroying the innocence of the Nambikwara, and introducing power relations into their communitarian way of life.

Derrida's book is designed to contest the privilege accorded to speech as natural and innocent. On the basis of Lévi-Strauss's own account, and without invoking any exterior information, Derrida shows that the Nambikwara are by no means as innocent as the story would have us believe. For instance, although their culture forbids the use of proper names, when the children quarrel, they betray the names of their antagonists to the anthropologist himself, who then has very little difficulty in extracting the names of everyone else. Violence, perfidy, and the willingness to oppress are already there, even among the children. The innocence of the Nambikwara is imaginary, no more than the anthropologist's dream of a purity lost to the West, but still present somewhere else, seen as subsisting outside the corruption of our own culture, in a purer, more *natural* society. Lévi-Strauss has reversed Western ethnocentric values in their conventional form. Instead of despising the Nambikwara, he idealizes them. But because his reversal of values stays within the same theoretical framework, it simply reproduces in another mode the ethnocentrism it was designed to challenge.

Derrida's project, however, is not to reverse the hierarchy, to privilege writing instead of speech. Instead, it is to demonstrate that the valued term, speech, is not exempt from the negative qualities attributed to writing. The 'proper' names of the Nambikwara, he argues, do not belong to individuals as if they were their 'property', the unique name denominating a unique person. On the contrary, names differentiate and classify – just like language, just like writing.

Derrida's real target here is not Lévi-Strauss himself, nor his anthropology, but what Derrida calls *phonocentrism*, the attribution to the human voice of a presence, an immediacy, and an innocence that is lost in writing. This, he urges, leads to the sentimentalization of a purity and innocence that never was: the oral community, all its members within earshot of each other, *authentic, present to itself.*

Deconstructing Saussure

Saussure, Derrida points out on the basis of an equally attentive deconstruction of the *Course in General Linguistics*, was as prone to phonocentrism as Lévi-Strauss – not surprisingly, since Saussure was heir to exactly the same Western philosophical tradition. Linguistics gives primacy to speech. In line with their Western heritage, specialists in linguistics still tend to see writing as secondary, no more than the transcription of oral exchange. Saussure's *Course*, Derrida demonstrates, denounces writing as variously monstrous, sinful, unnatural, perverse, tyrannical, pathological.

These are strong terms, and the inference must be that they betray a sense that something important is threatened by the existence of writing. But what?

Writing, Derrida explains, continues to signify in the absence of the writer. We can read Homer even though, if he was ever an individual at all, Homer has probably been dead for nearly three thousand years. The meaning of the *Odyssey* doesn't depend on our direct access to the world Homer described, even supposing it once existed, nor on the presence of Homer himself to confirm that we have understood his *true* meaning.

Of course, in the absence of Homer, we have no access to the meaning Homer may have intended to insert into the *Odyssey*. If we identifed the true meaning with *that*, it would follow that we could not read the *Odyssey* at all. But in practice, we self-evidently *can* follow the story of Odysseus' adventures, imagine the world he inhabits, and care about whether he finally finds his way home. We can *make sense* of this ancient epic. Writing, therefore, demonstrates that sense may always be something we make, that there may be no single true meaning, guaranteed by the word of the author, the *cogito* of consciousness, present to itself in thought, and uttered (outered, expressed) in the immediacy of unfallen speech.

In this way writing threatens the *logocentric* tradition of Western thought, the assumption that ideas come into being first, and seek expression in speech, which is then transcribed into writing. Logocentrism puts meaning at the centre, imagines that the signified exists in some realm of pure consciousness and then finds its outward form in language. Saussure's phonocentrism and his logocentrism, learned from the culture he inhabits, contradict the radical possibilities of his argument that meaning is an effect of the signifier, that the priority belongs to language itself, that we *learn* to mean.

If there are no pure, free-standing signifieds, we look in vain, Derrida explains, for the transcendental signified, the one true meaning that holds all the others in place, the foundational truth that exists beyond question and provides the answer to all subsidiary problems. Metaphysical systems of belief, laying claim to the truth, all appeal to some transcendental signified. For Christianity this is God, for the Enlightenment reason, and for science the laws of nature. But if we take meaning to be the effect of language, not its cause, these foundations lose their transcendental status. This does not reduce belief to the level of fiction, but it does undermine its anchorage in a truth beyond question.

In consequence, truth is no longer available as a source of authority. It does not follow from this that rockets do not reach the moon, or that bridges may suddenly fall down (unless the calculations were wrong in the first place). It simply implies a certain humility in

Q. Derrida is very hard to read. Why doesn't he write more simply? Doesn't he _want_ to communicate?

A. There are three reasons why we have difficulty in reading Derrida. The first is that he is a (Continental) philosopher, with a range of reference that is not widely available outside that tradition. Many of his more impenetrable remarks turn out to be allusions to Plato, Hegel, or Heidegger, and not obscure at all to people who have those writers at their fingertips, in a way that most of us don't. Second, he is very meticulous. What can seem repetitive and precious comes from a desire to be precise. But third, it is also important from the point of view of the case against logocentrism to demonstrate in practice that language is not transparent, not a pane of glass through which ideas are perceptible in their pure intelligibility. (On the other hand, the same mannerisms reproduced in the writings of his less gifted disciples can be very irritating indeed!)

relation to the reasoning that put them there. A good deal of science is hypothetical rather than certain; much medicine works without our knowing for sure why it does so. Success in practice does not always prove the accuracy of our theoretical map.

On the other hand, subjectivity is not an alternative. My personal beliefs are no guarantee of accuracy either. I might believe I could jump off 20-storey buildings and fly unaided – and I should probably find I was wrong.

What is in question is not whether we can fly, but access to a truth beyond language as the ground of knowledge, certainty.

Deconstruction, not critique

Traditional Western metaphysics advances on the basis of critique. You find the weakness in your antagonist's argument, and by this means show it to be false. In the tradition of Pope and Swift, you may then ridicule the argument, thereby persuading your reader to take your side against your antagonist. You go on to replace the previous position with your own views, which are then subject to critique in their turn.

Deconstruction, however, is not critique. Derrida treats Lévi-Strauss with respect, and his project is not to persuade us to repudiate Saussure, still less to ridicule him (though there are moments of comedy in his account of the sermon against the sin of writing delivered by the moralist from Geneva). Instead, he points out that Saussure's own book does not sustain the opposition between speech and writing it takes for granted and reiterates. On the contrary, the *Course* records (as an outrage) the invasion of the rejected writing into speech itself. Spelling, Saussure declares with horror, is changing pronunciation.

This is indeed often the case. Modern English examples include the introduction of a pronounced 't' into 'often', which formerly rhymed with 'soften'; the increasing pronunciation of 'again' to rhyme with 'Spain'; and even 'mayor' as two syllables. Speech is repeatedly modified by writing: the other invades the selfsame. Neither speech nor writing has logical priority: the two are not antithetical; we learn to signify from both.

Sonnet 18

Shakespeare's Sonnet 18, 'Shall I compare thee to a summer's day?', is one of his most popular poems. People read it out at weddings (though not as often as Sonnet 116) in lyrical celebration of an ideal romance. Will writes it for Viola in John Madden's film *Shakespeare in Love* (1998).

The poem seems to turn on a binary comparison between the beloved and the summer's day, in which the beloved is always the privileged term: 'Thou art more lovely and more temperate'. By contrast with the loved one, the weather is never quite right: 'Rough winds do shake the darling buds of May'; the temperature is either too hot or too cold. Besides, the products of the season are perfect only for a moment, while 'Thy eternal summer shall not fade'.

But what is the condition of this timeless perfection? Writing! The beloved is immune to decline and death only 'When in eternal lines to time thou grow'st'. The poem itself, it turns out, is what endows the mortal human being with immortality: 'So long as men can breathe, or eyes can see, / So long lives this, and this gives life to thee'. Sonnet 18, in other words, celebrates its own power to confer eternity.

The binary opposition, then, is not quite as simple as it first appeared. 'Thou' and the summer day, distinguished as antithetical, now appear on the same side of a line that divides mortality from poetry. All that lives is transitory, including the beloved: 'Every fair from fair sometime declines'. Just like the summer day, the living object of the poet's desire will, after all, fade and die: eternity belongs only to the poem and the poem's inscription of love.

But if love and summer resemble one another after all, in contrast to writing, which alone has immortal powers, what are we to make of the excess heat and cold of the summer day? Are they also properties the season shares with human love? Does the Sonnet imply that love too is very rarely, in practice, just right? And the rough winds that shake the darling buds? Are they, perhaps, sexy? Or at least tempestuous, the element of passion that makes love itself anything but 'temperate'?

The other invades the selfsame. The qualities of the repudiated summer day return to inhabit the romance they seemed designed to define by contrast.

What exactly, then, does Sonnet 18 claim? You are better than a summer's day, since you won't fade now that I've written this poem? Or, alternatively, you are mortal, like a summer's day, and won't fade if – and only if – I immortalize you in my poem? Who is in control here – the 'lovely' but mutable object of desire, or the desiring but life-giving poet? Or is the Sonnet a dramatization of a miniature power struggle, the sequence of implied threats and promises that goes on just below the surface of so many passionate relationships? Exactly how idealistic *is* this lyrical text? What is the *truth* of Sonnet 18? Perhaps it's undecidable?

Differance

Arguably, that element of undecidability, so common in Shakespeare's plays as well as the sonnets, and the deferral by the signifier of a single, determinable thematic meaning, or logos, plays a part in the continuing fascination of his work for us now, four centuries after its composition.

Derrida goes on to examine the implications of what survives in

Saussure's work if we take out the logocentrism implied by his phonocentrism, the residual privilege accorded to ideas and the voice. Meaning, Derrida concludes, is always the effect of the *trace*, paradoxically, of the other in the selfsame.

How do we define nature? Not by reference to flowers and trees, probably, since they are found in parks and can be cultivated, but as wildness, the absence of culture. By reference, in other words, to the term that is excluded by and from nature itself. And yet it is precisely from within culture that we are able to identify nature at all. The one term cannot be excluded from the meaning of the other. Meaning depends on difference.

It also, Derrida proposes, invokes differance (with an 'a'). If the signifier *differs* from another signifier, it also *defers* the meaning it produces. (English cannot capture the French pun or homonym: *différer* is both to differ and to defer.) That is to say, the signifier takes the place of the signified. Logocentrism imagines there is a pure concept, an idea. But where is this to be found? The signifier supplants it. Only the signifier is present in writing or speech: the imagined presence of the meaning as pure idea is deferred, pushed away and postponed, relegated by the signifier, which is all we can bring before us, or isolate for inspection.

Differance, a process, not an action we perform or undergo, neither active nor passive (like other terms ending in 'ance': assistance, resonance), is the only source of meaning. But differance has no content; it does not name any kind of presence or transcendence. It is not a concept. Indeed, it is not even a word.

In an essay on 'Differance', Derrida demonstrates that the term he has invented on the basis of the French homonym is also an instance of deconstruction, and a kind of ironic tribute to Saussure. It is impossible in speech, he reiterates, to use the term without explicitly invoking the spelling. You cannot, he insists, *hear* the difference between 'difference' and 'differance' (or *différence* and *différance*). The only way to make the distinction evident in speech is to say 'differance (with an a)'. Writing is triumphantly shown to invade the act of speaking. (Unfortunately, one of Derrida's translators left the word in French. His English-speaking admirers miss the point, however, when they deliver the word in an imitation of French pronunciation.)

Differance, neither a signifier (until Derrida used it) nor a signified (since it conjures up no imagined presence) is, nevertheless, the only origin of meaning. Not *full* (of an idea), nor *empty* (since it is intelligible), not foundational, since it cannot be appealed to as a guarantee of truth, differance is, all the same, what enables us to understand each other – to the degree that we do.

The strange case of Richard Mutt

What are the implications of all this? How, in practice, does deconstruction affect our understanding of the world? Let us give some thought to the case of Richard Mutt.

In April 1917 the American Society of Independent Artists held an exhibition. Modernism was in full swing, and this was a radical group, determined not to allow academic values to determine what counted as art. According to the rules of the Society, any artist of any nationality could be a member. The slogan for the exhibition was 'No jury, no prizes'. In order to avoid even the most unintentional hierarchy, Marcel Duchamp, an influential member of the Independents, is said to have suggested that the works should be hung in alphabetical order, starting with a letter drawn from a hat. For this inventive idea he was elected chair of the hanging committee.

The Independents drew the line, however, at an entry submitted by Richard Mutt, a readymade urinal, turned on its side and named *Fountain*. *Fountain* was not shown, and Marcel Duchamp promptly resigned his place on the committee, in support of artistic

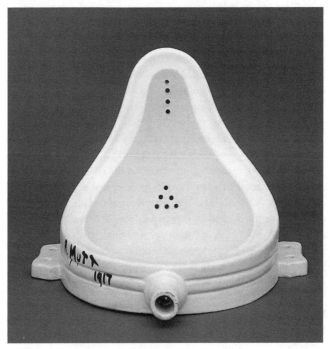

8. Is it art? Marcel Duchamp's *Fountain*.

freedom. The following month, the second issue of Duchamp's journal, *The Blind Man*, carried an unsigned editorial defending *Fountain*, and the cover displayed a photograph of the object itself by Alfred Stieglitz, the prestigious New York photographer and gallery-owner who had shown America the work of Rodin and Matisse, Cézanne and Toulouse-Lautrec. The photograph revealed an elegantly shadowed but clearly recognizable upturned urinal, signed 'R. Mutt 1917'.

As is now well known, R. Mutt was Marcel Duchamp, and *Fountain* was to become one of the most highly prized works of the 20th century. All that remains of the original, which was never shown, is the photograph, signifier of a signifier, the image of a 'work' which involved no work at all, by an artist who did not exist. Much later, Duchamp authorized a number of 'copies', now displayed in Paris, London, New York, and elsewhere. These copies were not exact replicas of the first *Fountain*, or each other. The lost original is infinitely deferred, supplanted by the copies. The Tate Modern in London displays a version of 1964, and a facsimile of *The Blind Man* is also on show in a glass case.

Thierry de Duve has argued that Duchamp's work in general, and *Fountain* in particular, mark a turning-point in aesthetics. Duchamp's readymades call into question the criteria of art. Was it art, this object which could hardly be described as beautiful, at least by conventional standards? Was it art, if it could be bought readymade and required no skill to produce? Was it art if it rejected all notion of expression or creativity? And finally, was it art if, as the work of a painter, it repudiated both paint and canvas, and yet, while standing firm in three dimensions, bore no other resemblance to existing sculpture either?

In 1917 the American Society of Independent Artists said no. But two generations later the art world resoundingly said yes, and there are copies of *Fountain* all over the world.

Who was right? Is there a correct answer? Not really: the question is probably undecidable, since the definition of art is not subject to legislation. Is the decision 'subjective', then? You can make up your own mind.

Yet in practice, however personal and individual it may feel, your choice depends on meaning, which is not subjective but conventional, and the condition of subjectivity itself. What is at stake in this instance is the meaning of 'art'. If you define art in terms of beauty, skill, or creativity, your answer has to be no; if you define it as what the art world calls art, or what the artist decides to call art, or what *anyone* chooses to call art, your answer must be yes.

So the question is linguistic, and the debates about what constitutes art are in the end debates about language. Who defines terms? Who has the right to decide what they mean? Can anyone finally and definitively say what art *is*? Poststructuralism would say not. The meaning, the concept, the truth of art is always differed and deferred by the signifier. 'Art' as pure idea cannot be made present to consciousness. *Fountain* both poses the question and stands in the way of any final, indisputable answer.

It is no solution, then, to argue that *Fountain* strips the signifier 'art' of all meaning. On the contrary, the word continues to mean, even if it means differently from different points of view. And for those who include *Fountain* in the category of art, the meaning of the term is irreversibly changed. Non-art (the readymade, the urinal) invades art (creative and uplifting); the trace of the other appears in the selfsame; and from then on, at least, the meaning of art has become undecidable. Art is no longer a pure concept to which we can appeal in order to judge Andy Warhol's *Brillo Boxes* or Tracey Emin's *Bed*. But then, perhaps it never was.

The implications of undecidability

Saussure's diagrams of the sign as a self-contained oval, with a line across the middle dividing signifier from signified, might give the impression that each signifier brings with it its own inseparable, single meaning. Deconstruction undoes that impression, pushes meaning towards undecidability, and in the process democratizes language. Binary oppositions do not hold, but can always be undone. The trace of otherness in the selfsame lays all oppositions open to deconstruction, leaving no pure or absolute concepts that can be taken as foundational. Meanings, not only the meaning of 'art' but of 'democracy' itself, or 'terrorism', or 'human rights', for example, are not individual, personal, or subjective, since they emanate from language. But they are not given in nature or guaranteed by any existing authority either.

At the same time, meanings are lived. Art fetches high prices, democracy is invoked to justify wars, and terrorists are hunted down. Human rights are a utopian aspiration and not, in most parts of the world, a reality. But they motivate legally binding decisions.

If meanings are not given or guaranteed, but lived all the same, it follows that they can be challenged and changed. And this is so not just for authority figures. If meaning is a matter of social convention, it concerns and involves all of us.

The implications of the poststructuralist analysis of signifying practice are the theme of the final chapter.

Chapter 5
Dissent

Programmed?

One common misreading of poststructuralist theory claims that it deprives us of the power to choose or to take action as agents in our own lives. This is binary thinking again: if the subject is an effect of meaning, if we are not the free, unconstrained origin of our own beliefs and values, so the story goes, we must be no better than artifical intelligences, programmed outside ourselves to act according to patterns determined elsewhere.

This is not how most poststructuralist thinkers have argued, however. Deconstruction implies, on the contrary, that meanings are not given unalterably in advance, but can be changed. Foucault stresses throughout his work the possibility of resistance, since power is always power *over* something or someone capable of disobeying. (No one claims power over turnips.) In Foucault's model, power is mobile, flexible, transferable. Both his position and Derrida's, in their distinct ways, imply choice and responsibility, ethical and political. Slavoj Žižek and Jean-François Lyotard in different ways take conflict for granted and assume that we choose sides.

Responsibility

Much of Derrida's later work has been concerned with ethics, the problem of right action in a world without foundational truths to constitute a ground for choice. Religions, in contrast, depend on such grounding. They determine what we ought to do by appealing in the last instance to the will of God, as revealed to priests or prophets in sacred signs. The will of God is in this sense taken as universal and ultimate, a pure and absolute reality beyond which human enquiry cannot hope to go. Secular beliefs might well find another ultimate reality to occupy the same structural position of authority: reason, for example, or the moral law, or perhaps the laws of nature. Such metaphysical values are taken as ultimate foundations on which all other values depend.

But if values emanate from language, and language divides the world differently from culture to culture, there can be no appeal to a universal, grounding reality. The will of God might or might not exist but, as history has shown, it seems in practice to be a site of considerable struggle, since both sides in a conflict commonly claim it for their cause. (One of the critical issues of the 21st century may well turn out to be whether it is more correctly interpreted by East or West.) Something similar goes for reason and nature. They are often cited, in the event, as supporting opposite points of view: feminist and anti-feminist, gay and homophobic.

Can there be, then, an ethics of deconstruction, an ethics without metaphysics? Derrida's own work is sceptical but also, he insists, 'affirmative'. If, on the one hand, the element of the other in the selfsame, the difference within cultures, languages, subjects, undermines both totalitarianism and nationalism, as well as all other attempts to bring societies or groups into line with a single identity, it does not, on the other hand, he argues, do away with the responsibility to take account of that very situation. Values not only have a history, they also differ *from themselves*. They can therefore be changed in the future, if not in the light of a fixed idea (or Idea) of the good, at least in the hope that the trace of an alternative inscribed in them might one day be realized. Derrida calls this way of thinking 'messianicity': not the promise of a specific messiah, who would fulfil an individual scripture, Christian, say, or Islamic, but the hope of a different future 'to come' (*avenir, à venir*).

Heroism

Deconstruction, then, is not incompatible with moral or political choice. Could there be an ethics of psychoanalysis?

In Lacan's view, since neurosis stems from repression, and neurosis is destructive, it follows that we should never give up on our desire. This proposition, it turns out, is neither as simple nor as hedonistic as it sounds. It certainly does not legitimate helping yourself to whatever you (think you) want, because desire is always unconscious, and the object of our conscious wishes is only a stand-in for something unrecognized, however much we seem consciously to want *that*, and only that.

According to Lacan, the primordial object is always lost to the subject. The first object of the libido in Freud, as everyone knows, is the mother. For Lacan, however, the Mother (capital M) is not a person, but a structural position. In Lacan's account, this maternal love-object is lost in the real, from which the world of signifiers tends to sever us, but which, at the same time, we continue to inhabit, as contradictory organisms-in-culture. Organisms that we are, we cannot escape the real; on the other hand, we cannot return to it – except in death. But death would dissolve both the subject and its desire. The lost object in the inextricable real beckons with the promise of immeasurable enjoyment, but would deliver only dissolution. Never giving up on your desire is in this sense dangerous. Lacan perceives heroism as the pursuit of the lost object – whatever the cost.

His example in the Seminar of 1959–60 is Antigone. Lacan has no time for what he dismissively calls 'the goods'. These 'goods' are duty, self-sacrifice, working for the good of others on the assumption that you know what that is, and, above all, good sense, as orthodox society understands that term. Antigone has no time for the goods either. King Creon has decreed that the corpse of her brother, the traitor Polynices, should remain unburied, as an example to others. Antigone, without extenuating the treason, is driven to give Polynices proper burial, simply because he is her kin, because they shared a womb. She defies the law, the rules of good conduct, her obligations to her sister and her future husband, and, above all, good sense as society understands it, to bury her brother, knowing that the penalty is to be walled up in her own tomb – or, in Lacan's terms, to return alive to the real.

Like Freud, then, Lacan traces to the protagonist of a Greek tragedy his account of the drive that impels human beings beyond their conscious wishes. Lacan stresses the contradictory character of the compulsions that motivate us. Love of the lost object and the death drive are inextricably entwined with one another in desire. Antigone never gives up on hers. And although Lacan is often accused of misogyny, his heroic example is a woman.

Lacan's heroine had already been invested with mythic status in French culture. Jean Anouilh's influential *Antigone*, first performed in occupied Paris in 1944, was widely understood at the time as a debate about the merits of resistance – and Resistance. Lacan unfolded his less ambivalent, but equally complex, reading of the Sophoclean original 15 years later.

The same Seminar of 1959–60 refers repeatedly to weapons of mass destruction as a threat to human kinship, and can be read as offering a theoretical account of the conflicting compulsions that would prevent and incite their use: love on the one hand and, on the other, the death drive projected outwards as aggression. Elsewhere in the world, this was also a time of vigorous activity to counter the equally vigorous human impulse towards destruction. The British

Campaign for Nuclear Disarmament was set up in 1958, with Bertrand Russell as its first president.

Sublimation

Mercifully, desire does not always require so much of us as it does of Antigone. Freud attributed the existence of civilization to the process of sublimation, which transformed raw sexual drives into socially approved activities: artistic creation, for example. Lacan sees works of art as attempts to reinscribe the lost object. But sublimation is not only for artists. In most lives, Lacan believes, the drive is brought to serve the interests of civilization, taking the innocent form of making things, teaching, writing, or pursuing the impulse towards knowledge.

But desire impels us all, none the less, as a radical discontent, a dissatisfaction with things as we find them, a restlessness that can find one outlet among others in a commitment to social and political change.

Antagonism

Slavoj Žižek has adapted Lacan's account to produce a more directly political analysis of the relation between human beings and society. Žižek, who is one of the most energetic heirs of Lacanian theory, himself rejects the label 'poststructuralist' (energetically), since he associates it with Derrida and what he sees as an exclusive and probably frivolous preoccupation with the signifier. (Derrida, in turn, is notoriously hostile to Lacan, accusing him of smuggling foundationalism in again through the back door, to create what he calls a 'metaphysics of absence'. At least no one could accuse poststructuralism of uniformity!)

Is it legitimate, then, to discuss Žižek here? I have been using the term 'poststructuralism' to indicate a body of work that has developed from Saussure's move to prise the signifier away from direct reference to the world, investing language with its own momentum, its independent determinations. In that sense, Lacan is explicitly indebted to Saussure, and Žižek is equally explicitly indebted to Lacan. But 'poststructuralism' cannot lay claim (of course!) to a single, authorized meaning based on an ultimate reality or truth. The question of Žižek's poststructuralism, then, may be finally undecidable.

But if the correct designation of his position remains to be determined, his views themselves are certainly not to be ignored. Žižek derives from Lacan a divorce between the symbolic order and the real, and he sees the residue of the lost real as leaving in the unconscious a traumatic kernel that is projected outwards as antagonism. He thus makes explicit the Lacanian identification of unconscious desire with the death drive, but where Lacan stresses the possibility of sublimation, Žižek finds 'the sublime'. In Žižek's account, the real is conflated with the lost object as a structural absence, which is masked in social relations by a 'sublime' fantasy figure. This figure is demonized by social orthodoxy as the eradicable cause of what is in practice an ineradicable antagonism.

In other words, the death drive finds social 'objects' as stand-ins for its dangerous seductions. Society blames the demons it has created for its own inevitable tensions, and allows itself to believe that their elimination will make it whole. Cold War America in the 1950s targeted 'the communists'; Hitler's Germany chose the Jews. At other times, different figures can be made to occupy the same structural position: psychopaths, drug peddlers, paedophiles . . . There is every danger that in the 21st century the West will construct as its antagonist in this sense 'the Islamic fundamentalist', who can then be held accountable for global disunity.

The problem here is, of course, that even if the supposed enemy of the good could be eliminated, the actual antagonism that inhabits the individual and therefore society would remain, since in Žižek's view this is structural. Social and political theory, Žižek argues, need

Slavoj Žižek, 1949–

In his native Slovenia Žižek obtained degrees in sociology and philosophy, as well as a PhD in philosophy, before going on to take a doctorate in psychoanalysis in Paris. He excited international attention with *The Sublime Object of Ideology*, still in many ways the most cogent exposition of his views, published in London and New York in 1989. This was followed by a series of books in rapid succession, including *Looking Awry: An Introduction to Jacques Lacan through Popular Culture* (1991), *Enjoy Your Symptom! Jacques Lacan in Hollywood and Out* (1992), *The Metastases of Enjoyment: Essays on Woman and Causality* (1994), and *The Ticklish Subject* (1999).

The experience of reading Žižek can be breathless, exhilarating, and infuriating by turns. He writes with apparently equal relish – and equal wit – on Hegel and popular cinema, Lacan and Jewish jokes. The first impression may be anarchic, and this is part of the pleasure, but the argument is often more rigorous than it seems. Unlikely observations turn out to be telling. In 'Two Ways to Avoid the Real of Desire', for example, Žižek draws parallels between high modernist fiction and the popular detective stories that emerged at roughly the same time. Though they are usually seen as antithetical, one difficult, demanding, obscure, and the other easy, familiar, 'realist', in practice the two modes share a rejection of linear narrative, since both refuse to tell the story in the order in which the events are understood to have happened.

Žižek himself claims that he retains a commitment to truth and the transcendental subject, as well as to Marx alongside a secularized version of St Paul!

to take account of this antagonism, instead of setting out simply to suppress it, in the way of totalitarianism, or trying to civilize it, as liberal democracy does.

Dissension

In their different ways, both totalitarianism and liberalism seek to establish consensus, the one by eradicating opposition and the other by negotiating with it. This project, in the view of Jean-François Lyotard, is itself mistaken. What we need if things are to get better, he argues, is not consensus, but dissension. The commitment to consensus promotes a bland centrism, appoints the compromise candidate that no one really wants, satisfies nobody, and leaves things much as they are. Conversely, intellectual difference, inventiveness, lateral thinking, heterogeneity all promote modifications of the existing rules and conventions. Dissension challenges the status quo.

How is dissension to be actively fostered as disagreement but not

> **Q. But surely we need more consensus, not less? Haven't Western democracies set as their goal the kind of discussion that would resolve conflict and allow people of differing convictions to live in harmony?**
>
> **A. Tolerance slides easily towards indifference, as the efficiency of the economy becomes the only shared commitment. Similarly, compromise turns readily into complacency, when the familiar seems safer than the unknown. 'Neutrality', it often turns out, is not neutral at all, but sides with the way things are to avoid the dissension that might lead to change for the better. Consensus, then, may come into conflict with justice.**

violence? Where does the opportunity to construct and debate different views find its place within a poststructuralist account of human culture? Or what in the nature of signifying practice permits us to theorize the practices that resist culture's homogenizing imperative?

Language games

In answer, Lyotard appeals to Ludwig Wittgenstein's account of language as a series of 'games'. Utterances can be divided into various types, which depend on shared rules, and produce a relationship between the speakers, just as games require rules and generate a relationship between players. For instance, Lyotard explains, a statement of 'fact' places the person making the statement in the position of someone who *knows*, and the addressee as the person who agrees or disagrees. By contrast, a question reverses the roles: if I ask the way, I attribute knowledge to my interlocutor. (No wonder men find it harder to ask for directions than women do!) If I give an instruction, I lay claim to authority. My interlocutor can either accept this, or refuse it and disobey. In all these instances, the speaker implicitly either claims or cedes power, while the addressee either takes up or withholds the position offered. We can never predict with certainty the 'move' our interlocutor will make.

In this sense, then, Lyotard says, dialogue can be seen as a succession of manoeuvres, and 'to speak is to fight, in the sense of playing', though he hastens to add that we do not always play to win. There is also a pleasure to be gained from sheer linguistic inventiveness: telling jokes, recounting stories, producing slogans, making puns. Perhaps in these instances our opponent is conventional language itself.

Lewis Carroll's Humpty Dumpty would surely have agreed. His interpretation of 'Jabberwocky' is at least as linguistically inventive – and as engagingly nonsensical – as the poem itself. And he conducts the entire conversation with Alice as a series of moves. At one point he demands to return to the last remark but one. Not surprisingly, Alice cannot remember what it was. '"In that case we may start afresh," said Humpty Dumpty, "and it's my turn to choose a subject" – ("He talks about it just as if it was a game!" thought Alice).'

But Humpty Dumpty's creator would surely have agreed too. It is no accident that *Through the Looking Glass*, which consistently challenges the reader with riddles and linguistic conundrums, is structured in terms of a chess game.

In everyday exchanges language games need not be a matter of conscious intention. Lyotard's account is designed to describe what takes place, whether the speakers concerned know it or not. But the process could become conscious. By winning a round, replying unexpectedly, altering the terms of the debate, or dissenting from the dominant position, we can shift the power relations, however imperceptibly.

Nodal points

Powerless though we might seem to ourselves to be, everyone is located, Lyotard points out, in circuits of communication; we all occupy 'nodal points' to which messages are transmitted, and from which we re-transmit them. Interference with the message, however slight, changes the content, or the place of the addressee, and has the capacity to alter in the process the power relations it was designed to reaffirm.

Such modifications, as we know, take place all the time. You pass on an instruction, but reduce the urgency. The management demands a report on the low sales figures, and your response unexpectedly implicates their own mismanagement. Novels can invite a shift of sympathy, and so of allegiance: Jean Rhys retells Charlotte Brontë's story of Mr Rochester's mad wife from Bertha Mason's own point of

Jean-François Lyotard, 1924–98

The book that brought Lyotard to international – and controversial – attention was *The Postmodern Condition: A Report on Knowledge* (1979, tr. 1984), which defined the postmodern as 'incredulity toward metanarratives'. Lyotard's metanarratives, or 'grand narratives', are those totalizing accounts of the world that offer to explain everything, including 'little narratives', the familiar stories that represent our own culture to us. Little narratives – individual records, fictions, histories of particular moments – identify heroes and villains, and name the knowledges worth possessing. They represent inscriptions of shared meanings and values. At the same time, the values inscribed in these little narratives are often incommensurable with one another, demonstrating that culture is not homogeneous or uniform. Grand narratives, by contrast, reduce the little narratives to their own terms. Indeed, they reduce all history to a single trajectory: the progressive emergence of rational values, for instance; or, alternatively, 'development' towards the global market. The inevitable triumph of the working class was just such a metanarrative, and *The Postmodern Condition* has not been popular with Marxists.

Lyotard's own values are heterogeneity, the multiplication of difference, and the pursuit of the as-yet unknown by means of what he calls 'paralogy', a form of reasoning that either breaks the rules or invents new ones. *The Differend* (1983) argues that disputes between incommensurable positions cannot be resolved without injustice to one side or the other.

view; Jacqueline Rose rewrites Proust's *À la recherche du temps perdu* from Albertine's. When Baz Luhrmann moves the setting of his *William Shakespeare's Romeo + Juliet* (1996) from Renaissance Verona to Verona Beach, California, he turns a play about the conflict between romance and arranged marriage into the depiction of a high-tech, high-expenditure society that crushes innocence while offering an equally glittering, but ineffectual, religion as the only heart of a heartless world. At times of war, each side redefines the other's message: a 'war on terrorism' becomes a 'war against Islam', and in the process constitutes a rallying call to East against West.

The avant-garde

In an explicitly polemical essay, 'Answering the Question: What is Postmodernism?', Lyotard put forward a strong plea for continued artistic dissent. Cultures, he argued, need the challenge of new forms if they are not to settle into complacency or, worse, terror.

His target here is what he calls 'realism'. Realism, he claims, reaffirms the illusion that we are able to seize hold of reality, truth, the way things 'really' are. Photography, film, and television, offering themselves as windows onto the world, delivering 'the facts', are no more than the completion of the programme of ordering visual space that began with Renaissance painting.

In 15th-century Italy, painters began to depict the world according to the rules of fixed-point perspective. As long as all the lines understood to be parallel to the ground converged at a single vanishing point, and as long as objects were shown as diminished and foreshortened accordingly, three dimensions were miraculously inscribed on a two-dimensional canvas, and the 'truth' appeared in painting. But this 'truth' was the effect of geometry; it was an illusion. On condition that the viewer stood in exactly the right position, opposite the vanishing point and at the distance, scaled for size, of the painter from the scene, and as long as the picture was viewed with one eye closed, the illusion of truth was conjured out of a very skilful fiction.

Dutch realism of the 17th century rendered the world we believe we know with an exceptional level of accuracy. Pieter de Hooch shows space receding in and beyond a courtyard in Delft. He also includes in this domestic space three figures that realism places as belonging there, all of them female.

9. Pieter de Hooch's three-dimensional space encloses women.

Literary realism, meanwhile, also relied on the reader to 'recognize' the world it depicted with such persuasive touches of verisimilitude, and it too ordered the way things were perceived, addressed its account of the world to a single viewpoint, and made social relations make sense from there. A classic detective story begins with an enigma: who killed the victim, and why? By the end, we know the identity of the murderer and the motive for the crime (or if we don't, we feel cheated). But in delivering the explanation, the disclosure that makes everything clear, the story also reaffirms what is plausible as an account of human behaviour, what seems likely, 'realistic'. This commonly includes the idea that wickedness is finally brought to book.

Realism, Lyotard argues, protects us from doubt. It offers us a picture of the world that we seem to know, and in the process confirms our own status as knowing subjects by reaffirming that picture as true. Things are, human beings are, and, above all, *we* are just as we have always supposed.

Postmodernity, in Lyotard's account, specifies a different literary and artistic mode rather than a particular period. Duchamp's challenge to realism is intelligible as postmodern. 'You want realism?' Richard Mutt's urinal seemed to ask. 'I'll give you reality itself, a readymade urinal, exactly the kind you see every day'. Er, that is, the kind men see every day. Well, Western men, anyway. Reality itself, when you come to think of it, is also culturally relative.

At the beginning of the 20th century, experimental art and literature challenged the dominance of realism, proclaimed it the effect of a trick, and broke with its values to acknowledge the inaccessibility of the truth itself at the level of the signifier. One branch of the new experimentalism – Lyotard calls it 'modernism' – lamented the impossibility of truth and devoted itself to defining in stories and artworks a nostalgia for lost presence. The other, the postmodern, rejoiced in the freedom this impossibility conferred.

Postmodernism celebrates the capability of the signifier itself to create new forms and, indeed, new rules.

There is, of course, Lyotard concedes, a postmodernism of the market place, an eclecticism at the level of style which gives easy pleasure and makes big profits at the same time. But this aesthetics of the kitsch, the conviction that 'anything goes', is a long way from the challenge of the avant-garde, which stretches the possibilities of signifying practice.

As his main literary example, Lyotard invokes James Joyce. *Ulysses*, published in 1922, marked a departure from the 19th-century novel. In its account of a day in Dublin, the novel depicts events, but largely ignores plot and suspense – the conventional realist structure, in other words, of enigma leading to final disclosure. As an alternative, *Ulysses* offers dazzling wordplay and the pleasure of unexpected formulations, explicitly displaying language as a succession of games in which the main opponent is convention itself. Nor does *Ulysses* much resemble Homer's *Odyssey*, the work it continually alludes to and parodies: the brilliance of Joyce's ironic reinscription of the epic depends on that difference. *Ulysses* is overtly, jubilantly textual and intertextual. Its pleasures reside in the signifier, not in an imagined space on the other side of the writing.

Terror

The postmodern, or the avant-garde, refuses to conform to pre-existing rules. Instead, Lyotard argues, the postmodern artist and writer are working without rules, in order to discover what the rules governing their work *will have been*. The postmodern is both too early and too late: too early for the public, since it must be new; too late for the author, who cannot know in advance whether it will prove to be intelligible, pleasurable, or absurd. *Ulysses* was banned; now many see it as the greatest novel of the 20th century.

Duchamp's *Fountain* was rejected by the Independents; now authorized copies are priceless.

In this sense, the postmodern poses not only a challenge, but a question. 'What do you think?', it implicitly asks. Or, better, 'Are you able to think beyond the limits of what is already recognizable? Is it possible to acknowledge the hitherto unknown?'

Both Nazism and Stalinism deplored the avant-garde. National Socialism endorsed Classicism and pronounced modern art decadent; Stalin promoted Socialist Realism at the expense of the experimental forms that had developed immediately after the Revolution. Each regime believed that it possessed the truth, and that art should reaffirm that conviction by reproducing the reality the authorities defined as acceptable.

Lyotard associates the fantasy of possessing the truth with terror. The avant-garde is not just a matter of style. Because it poses questions, it undermines all certainties, including the certainty that you possess the truth – and are entitled to kill people in its name.

'A Postmodern Fable'

What is the appropriate genre for a postmodern narrative? There can be no rules in advance, of course, but only new forms, or old forms reappropriated for new purposes.

In 'A Postmodern Fable' Lyotard radically reinvents one of the oldest genres of all. Fables are conventionally consoling or explanatory. They find palatable ways of delivering moral truths or accounting for the origins of things. They provide answers to real questions, but they are by definition fictitious: they 'fabulate'. By contrast, Lyotard's postmodern instance of the genre does not offer much consolation; it provides no answers but poses a question; it fabulates very little, but reproduces the conclusions of modern science. And it begins at the end of the story:

What a Human and his/her Brain – or rather the Brain and its Human – would resemble at the moment when they leave the planet forever, before its destruction; that, the story does not tell. So ends the fable we are about to hear. The Sun is going to explode.

'A Postmodern Fable' asks whether 'we' can survive the inevitable explosion of the Sun four and a half billion solar years from now. All stars eventually extinguish themselves in a conflagration, and the Sun is no exception. It will go up in flames, taking the Earth with it. Will human beings escape?

The question might not seem particularly urgent or pressing: we have four and a half billion years to come up with an answer. But a happy ending may well presuppose that 'we' become something other than we are, beings capable of survival in circumstances quite different from those in which we evolved.

What are 'we'? Lyotard's fable replies that human beings are an effect of 'the fortuitous conjugation of various forms of energy', the molecular composition of the Earth's surface in conjunction with solar radiation, which led to the formation of living cells. There followed cell division, a form of birth and death, then sexual reproduction, natural selection, language . . . The postmodern fable thus explains the origins of things, after all. Its protagonist, however, is not a human being, understood as no more than an accidental effect, but energy itself.

According to Lyotard's futuristic fable, scientific resources were increasingly devoted to human survival beyond the end of the world. The human body, adapted to life on Earth, would need prosthetic remodelling or replacement in such a way that the brain would continue to work in a different environment. But what it would be like the story does not say.

Since this is a postmodern fable, the text includes its own

commentary on the story it tells. The fable, it points out, does not repudiate realism: on the contrary, it embraces information about the world that is scientifically verifiable. But it is not science. Instead, as fiction, it represents a special organization of language, which is itself a form of energy in a particularly complex state. Fiction involves imagination. Science and technology also involve imagination – to a high degree – but they are subject in the end to the criteria of truth: they submit their propositions to the test of verification or falsification.

Fables don't. They are entitled to leave the answers in suspense, releasing in the process the options for invention, discovery, paralogy on the part of the reader. We are invited to supply the ending we should like the story to have – and in the process to suppose ourselves superseded by something unimaginable.

What makes *this* fable postmodern, Lyotard argues, is its repudiation of the teleological structure of the grand narratives that characterize modernity. 'Modernity' begins, in this instance, with Christianity, which offers an archetypal grand narrative. According to the Christian account, the end of the world will reinstate the condition that was there at the beginning. The reign of God, in other words, will restore the relationship with human beings as it existed before the Fall. During the Enlightenment, secular grand narratives rewrote this story, promising for the benefit of human beings the restoration of the reign of nature, or the classless society – the original state of affairs before things went wrong.

Lyotard's postmodern fable has no place for the assumption that history is motivated by a design that works in the end for the good of the human subject. On the contrary, the fable treats time as a series of discontinuous states of energy, and the subject as a temporary effect, not a motive but an incidental by-product of a transitory condition of matter.

The fable is bleak, then, as befits a story told in line with postmodern uncertainty, the condition theorized by poststructuralism itself. But it is not pessimistic, since it leaves the future open. We are not at the mercy, it indicates, of a malignant force, any more than we are the creation of a benevolent designer. Instead, what is to become of us is to some degree in our hands. If the science produced by the effect of a 'fortuitous conjugation of various forms of energy' confirms the belief that the world will end in due course, that same science is capable of intervening in the interests of a possible future for some unimagined version of the Brain and its Human.

The end of the story remains, then, to be decided. Moreover, the story is, precisely, a fable, a fabulation, which asks, Lyotard says, 'not that it be believed, but that we reflect on it'.

Poststructuralism and reflection

What poststructuralism offers is, in the end, an opportunity and a cause for reflection. It proposes a lexicon and a syntax, which is to say a vocabulary and an indication of the ways words legitimately relate to each other. But the language poststructuralism puts forward – on the basis, of course, in the first instance, of a study of language itself – is more useful in prompting the uncertainty of questions than in delivering the finality of answers.

The project is that the questions might replace the bewildering alternatives of the intellectual market place with a more sharply focused undecidability that specifies the options while leaving them open to debate. In that respect, in its emphasis on the degree to which we make our own story, subject to certain specifiable constraints, poststructuralism is at once sceptical towards inherited authority and affirmative about future possibilities.

Above all, it asks, like Lyotard's fable, that we reflect on it.

References

Chapter 1

The most useful translation of Ferdinand de Saussure's *Course in General Linguistics* is by Wade Baskin (Fontana, 1974). (The Roy Harris translation does not use the vocabulary poststructuralism was to take up, and so fails to indicate how influential the book was to be.) The crucial points are made in the chapter on 'Linguistic Value' (pp. 111–22). Julia Kristeva explains the semiotic in her *Revolution in Poetic Language*, tr. Margaret Waller (Columbia University Press, 1984), pp. 19–106. 'The Death of the Author' can be found in Roland Barthes, *Image-Music-Text* (Fontana, 1977), pp. 142–8.

Chapter 2

For 'Soap Powders and Detergents' and 'The Face of Garbo', see Roland Barthes, *Mythologies* (Vintage, 1993), pp. 36–8 and 56–7. Skincare is discussed in the subsequent collection, *The Eiffel Tower and Other Mythologies* (University of California Press, 1997), pp. 47–9. Saussure defines semiology in the *Course* (pp. 16–17). Karl Marx and Friedrich Engels, *The German Ideology* is available in several editions. The most useful passages are also reproduced in David McLellan (ed.), *Karl Marx: Selected Writings* (Oxford University Press, 1977). Louis Althusser's essay, 'Ideology and Ideological State Apparatuses (Notes Towards an Investigation)' appears in his *Lenin and Philosophy and Other Essays* (New Left Books, 1971), pp. 121–73. Roland Barthes discusses the in-difference of structuralism in his *S/Z* (Jonathan Cape, 1975), p. 3.

Chapter 3

The hermaphrodite's story is told in Michel Foucault (ed.), *Herculine Barbin* (Pantheon, 1980). Julia Kristeva's comments on our own inevitable foreignness are from her *Strangers to Ourselves* (Columbia University Press, 1991), pp. 189, 191. René Descartes defines the *cogito* in his *Discourse on Method* (Penguin, 1968), pp. 53–4.

Chapter 4

Jacques Derrida deconstructs Lévi-Strauss in 'The Violence of the Letter', *Of Grammatology* (Johns Hopkins, 1997), pp. 101–40. The account of Saussure and differance precedes this (pp. 27–73).

Chapter 5

Lacan reads *Antigone* in *Seminar 7: The Ethics of Psychoanalysis* (Routledge, 1992), pp. 241–87. Lyotard's theory of dialogue as conflict appears in *The Postmodern Condition: A Report on Knowledge* (Manchester University Press, 1984), pp. 10, 15. 'Answering the question: What is postmodernism?' is appended to the same volume. The fable is one of his *Postmodern Fables* (University of Minnesota Press, 1997), pp. 83–101.

Further reading

Introductions necessarily simplify the issues, in some cases to the point where they are barely recognizable. Among those that don't, and from a literary-critical point of view, Andrew Bennett and Nicholas Royle offer a lively alternative to the usual summaries and digests in *An Introduction to Literature, Criticism and Theory* (Prentice Hall Europe, 1999). As far as specific authors are concerned, Malcolm Bowie can be trusted on *Lacan* (Fontana, 1991), as can Dylan Evans, *An Introductory Dictionary of Lacanian Psychoanalysis* (Routledge, 1996). Geoffrey Bennington's *Interrupting Derrida* (Routledge, 2000) makes some concessions to the reader. Bill Readings, *Introducing Lyotard: Art and Politics* (Routledge, 1991) is excellent. I have put some of the theories to work in *Desire: Love Stories in Western Culture* (Blackwell, 1994).

By far the best way to find out more about poststructuralism, however, is to read the texts themselves. Some (but by no means all) of these are difficult at first, but it gets easier – like learning a language. Roland Barthes's *Mythologies* (Vintage, 1993) is a pleasure to read, as is his *A Lover's Discourse: Fragments* (Penguin, 1990). Michel Foucault's most widely influential works are not particularly obscure: *The History of Sexuality, Volume 1* (Allen Lane, 1979) and *Discipline and Punish* (Penguin, 1979). Slavoj Žižek's work is delightful (though harder than it seems). Try *Looking Awry: An Introduction to Jacques Lacan Through Popular Culture* (MIT, 1991), or *Enjoy Your Symptom! Jacques Lacan in Hollywood and Out* (Routledge, 1992).

Derrida's *Monolingualism of the Other; or, The Prosthesis of Origin* (Stanford University Press, 1998) is approachable, as is *Positions* (Athlone, 1987). After that, as far as Derrida is concerned, it's a question of what interests you. Among his late works, *Aporias* (Stanford University Press, 1993) is about death; *Specters of Marx* (Routledge, 1994) argues that we can't afford to forget Marxism (and analyses the opening scenes of *Hamlet*); and *The Gift of Death* (University of Chicago Press, 1995) is about ethics (not death, except incidentally).

As for Lyotard, *The Postmodern Explained to Children* (Turnaround, 1992) sounds easier than it is. *The Inhuman* (Polity, 1991) is a collection of essays, some more polemical than others. My favourite? 'Can Thought Go On Without a Body?' (pp. 8–23).

Glossary

Author: traditional 'explanation' of the text; a means of imposing limits on the proliferation of meaning.

bourgeoisie: class owning the forces of production in capitalism.

citationality: the process of quotation, reiteration, allusion that makes signifying practices intelligible.

culture: the inscription in stories, rituals, customs, objects, and practices of the meanings in circulation at a specific time and place.

deconstruction: analysis of the invasion of the excluded, differentiating other into the selfsame (see *trace*).

differance: the deferral of the imagined concept or meaning by the *signifier*, which takes its place and in the process relegates it beyond access; the only (but always non-positive) 'origin' of meaning.

drive: the psychic representative of an instinct.

ideology: forms of social exchange justifying the dominance of the ruling class (Marx); assumptions, values, the obvious, inscribed in material practices (Althusser).

logocentrism: supposition that meanings have priority over the *signifier*, that language is the expression of a prior concept existing as pure intelligibility.

metanarrative (or **grand narrative**): a comprehensive, totalizing story, which accounts for everything and reduces all little stories to its terms.

metaphysics: the quest for underlying realities, the ultimate foundations on which analysis can rest.

Other: the *symbolic order*, which exists outside us and is the condition of becoming a *subject* (Lacan).

phonocentrism: privilege accorded to the voice or speech.

real: the unnameable; that which resides beyond the reach of the *signifier*; lost organic being (Lacan).

semiology: the study of signifying practice; analysis of the inscription of meanings in culture.

semiotic, the: sounds and rhythms that disrupt 'thetic' (rational) thematic meaning (Kristeva).

signifier: a sound, image, written shape, object, practice, or gesture invested with meaning.

structuralism: identification of universal structures underlying culture, usually as binary oppositions; belief that human beings are the effect of structures that escape their awareness.

subject: that which is capable of signifying practice and thus agency, choice; at the same time, the effect of subjection to the *symbolic order*.

symbolic order: the discipline which is the condition of the ability to symbolize or signify; the order of language and *culture*.

trace: the residue in the *signifier* of the excluded, differentiating term which constitutes the only source of its meaning.

transcendental signified: the (imagined) founding meaning that would hold all other meanings in place (see *metaphysics*).

Index

Expand your collection of
VERY SHORT INTRODUCTIONS

Visit the
VERY SHORT
INTRODUCTIONS
Web site

www.oup.co.uk/vsi

➤ **Information** about all published titles

➤ News of **forthcoming books**

➤ **Extracts** from the books, including titles
not yet published

➤ **Reviews** and views

➤ **Links** to other **web sites** and main
OUP web page

➤ Information about **VSIs in translation**

➤ **Contact** the editors

➤ **Order** other **VSIs** on-line